LEARNING KOREAN WITH A SMILE

READING&WRITING HANGEUL

ADRIAN PERRIG

AH-YEONG YU

HEEJO LEE

YEON YIM

Für Heidi Perrig - Adrian Perrig
하이디 페릭을 위해 – 아드리안 페릭

For King Sejong - Ah-yeong Yu
그리고 환상의 커플인 엄마,아빠 감사합니다 – 유아영

To my parents in a peach orchard - Heejo Lee
엄마, 아빠 사랑해요 – 막내아들 회조 올림

For Clara Moon - Yeon Yim
어머니께 – 임정연

ACKNOWLEDGMENT

We are greatly indebted to numerous people for helping us with this book. In the early stages of Adrian's Korean studies, he would like to thank Hyun Jin Kim and Juyeong Lee for patiently supporting his initial inquiries. In the early stages of the book, we would like to thank Chloe Fung for her comment's and suggestions, in particular for her support for diagram-based depiction of concepts. We also thank Eunah Kim for her suggestions for improvements. Lili Avery, Marco Gruteser, Collin Jackson, and Hyun Jin Kim have read versions of the book and provided valuable feedback that helped us greatly improve the book. Thanks to everyone!

Moving forward, we are looking forward to hearing comments and suggestions on how to further improve this book. With your encouragement and support, we anticipate to publish a complete Korean study book, to enable you to study the language with a smile!

For comments & suggestions
Email us at : info@smile-korean.com
Visit us at : www.smile-korean.com

CONTENTS

"WHEN YOU FIRST LEARN KOREAN, YOU WILL FIRST SMILE, BUT EVENTUALLY YOU WILL CRY!"

These were the "encouraging" words of my first Korean teacher, intended to test my determination, possibly to ensure that she's not wasting her time on someone who will give up after the second lesson. I thought I could see through her plan and answered with confidence "No problem, I can handle it!"

As I soon found out, she was not trying to play a trick on me, but she was simply stating a fact. Indeed, starting to learn Korean starts with learning reading and writing. Although seemingly cryptic at first sight, one can learn the phonetic writing system within a few hours and even start decoding and pronouncing simple words after a few minutes. So initially, I was smiling so big that the corners of my mouth were touching my ears.

After a short while, however, reality sunk in. I realized that learning Korean is quite difficult and seemingly basic concepts appeared impenetrable and confusing at first. Fortunately, thanks to my excellent teachers, we figured out simple tricks that could cut through the jungle of complexity, and help avoid the most tears of desperation.

With an engineering background, one would like to understand "why things are the way they are." Rote memorization doesn't work well for everyone. Moreover, once a pattern becomes clear and makes sense, it is much easier to understand, remember, and apply. Consequently, our goal was to find simple explanations for concepts to simplify your studies.

In this book, we will help you unlock the secrets of Hangeul (the Korean script) reading and writing. Within two hours, you can learn the basic characters and pronounce many words. So the beginning is really easy. However, a significant amount of complexity needs to be overcome to master the numerous special cases and exceptions. The best way to use this book (and keep you sane) is to solidly learn the basics and initially only skim over the more complex concepts. As you make progress learning Korean, we recommend you to revisit the complex pronunciations as they arise, and internalize them over time. Throughout this book, we will point out and encourage you to focus on the most important concepts, to save the less frequently used concepts for your later studies to becoming a Korean master.

A major difference of this book is that we do not stop short teaching printed Hangeul. In our own experience, one can carefully learn nicely typed Hangeul yet be dumbfounded or even dumbstruck not being able to decipher some newspaper text, artistically typed characters, or especially handwritten characters. Fortunately, a small amount of practice gets one far — a minimal amount of training enables one to decipher all but the wildest writing styles.

Similarly, typing Hangeul on keyboards can be intimidating at first, especially on cell phones, but with an ounce of knowledge one can prevent a pound of frustration.

Let's get started, and we hope that we will help you learn Korean reading and writing while retaining your smile!

INTRODUCTION

In this book, we will study how to read and write Hangeul, the Korean character script. Compared to other Asian languages, the Korean script is simple to learn: in as few as two hours of study, you can already pronounce the majority of characters and read simple words. This is exciting, as this enables you to pronounce any Korean writing which you will likely encounter even outside Korea.

1. HISTORY OF HANGEUL

Hangeul (한글, often written as Hangul) was completed in 1443
by a group of scholars under King Sejong the Great.
They created the characters from a research of ancient patterns
based on an orthographic approach to the sounds of human voice.

CREATION OF HANGEUL

Before the creation of Hangeul, the majority of people such as farmers, fishers, hunters, butchers, craftsmen, or clothiers could not read or write : only members of the highest class were literate. Despite the substantial difference between Korean and Mandarin, Chinese characters had been used to write Korean, which King Sejong observed as a cumbersome condition.

To help people read and write regardless of their age, gender, education level, or social position, King Sejong decided to create simple letters that anyone can learn.

King Sejong said :
"Until now, we have not had letters proper for our language. I feel sorry for my people who cannot express their thoughts in writing. So I release 28 new letters myself. I name them 'Hun Min Jeong Eum' (훈민정음 : The Proper Sounds for the Education of the People). My people shall be able to learn them and use them every day."

Although Hangeul faced opposition by some of the literate elite after its creation (possibly for fear of losing their superiority if everyone could read and write), it eventually entered popular culture as Sejong had intended, being used especially by women and writers of popular fiction.

·다	롤	:어	:몯	ꥱ	ㄴㅣ	·이	셔	나
:히	맹	엿	ᅙᅩᇰ	·촘	ㄹ	런	ㄹ	·랏
·ᅅᅧ	ㄱ	·비	·노	:내	·고	젼	ᄼ	:말
:수	ㄴ	너	·미	제	져	·ᄎ	못	ᄴ
·ᄫᅵ	ㄴㅣ	·겨	하	·ᄠ	·ᅘᅩᇰ	·로	·디	·미

Hun Min Jeong Eum (1446)

After Hangeul was released in 1446, it took more than 400 years until its official usage.

Hangeul was finally adopted in official documents for the first time in 1894. And elementary school texts began using Hangeul in 1895. Korea, both South and North, now uses Hangeul as the sole official written language. As a concise and powerful writing system, Hangeul helps educate people to learn and write easily, and Korea has become one of the nations with the lowest illiteracy rates in the world.[1]

Hangeul is combinational; it can express 8800 sounds, while other East Asian alphabets have individual sounds for each symbol, only representing 300-400 sounds on average.

An interesting fact is that the town of Bau-Bau in Sulawesi, Indonesia, selected Hangeul in 2009 to write the Cia-Cia language.[2] Who knows, maybe Hangeul will become one of the universal phonetic languages in the world!

---

1 List of countries by literacy rate, included in the United Nations Development Programme (UNDP) Report 2011
2 http://en.wikipedia.org/wiki/Cia-Cia_language#Orthography

ANCIENT TRACES OF HANGEUL

Although it is a well-known story that King Sejong created Hangeul, there are historical traces showing that the creation of Hangeul was done by many scholars as a team.

Several history books written in 15th-16th century indicate that when working on Hangeul, King Sejong and his scholars may have referred to other languages to find the general patterns. According to 'Yong-jae Chong-hwa' (1525), King Sejong had a department of Eon-mun[3] consisting of several scholars to make Hangeul. 'Sejong-shillok' (1454) states that Hangeul was to "pursue the classics."

There are widely different views on understanding the actual meaning of 'classics.' Some argue that Hangeul is based on the Phags-pa script which has visual similarities. Some argue that Hangeul adopts the phonologic system of Sanskrit. Some argue that it is the philosophy of China which had been the main stream in Asia.

Whatever it may be, we should give the honor of Hangeul to all who attributed on its creation. King Sejong's real name was Do Lee, as a great leader. Sukju Shin, Sammun Seong, Inji Chung, Paeng-nyeon Park, Heean Kang, Seonro Lee, Su-seong Kim and Hang Choi are known to be the essential contributing members, but there could be other contributors as well.

Next, we look at some of the ancient writing systems that King Sejong and his scholars may have used for inspiration when they created Hangeul.

---

3 Hangeul was called 'Eon-mun' until 1910, which means 'phonetic script' in Korean.

PHAGS-PA SCRIPT

The Phags-pa script[4] is an alphabet made by Tibetan Lama Zhogoin Qoigyai Pagba, as a unified script for the literary languages of the Chinese Yuan Dynasty (1271-1368). Gari Ledyard[5], an honorary professor at Colombia University, claims that Hangeul symbols 'ㄱ, ㄷ, ㄹ, ㅂ, ㅈ' originated from the Phags-pa script, as they resemble to 'ꡂ, ꡊ, ꡘ, ꡎ, ꡛ' in Tibetan today. They may be cognate with 'Γ, Δ, Λ, Β' in the Greek alphabet, one of the earliest alphabets remaining in use, and also with 'C/G, D, L, B' in the Latin alphabet.

AHIRU SCRIPT

The Ahiru script is one of the 'Jindai-moji'[6] found in Japan. Jindai-moji is a series of ancient characters presented by several scholars in Japan around the Mid-Edo period (1603-1808), that was said to have existed before Chinese characters were introduced to Japan. The Japanese academic society today regards the Jindai-moji as forgeries, claiming that they are just being used as materials of fictions. While many of them resemble earlier forms of Chinese characters, the Ahiru script is the only one that resembles Hangeul.

4 http://en.wikipedia.org/wiki/Phags-pa_script
5 http://en.wikipedia.org/wiki/Gari_Ledyard
6 http://en.wikipedia.org/wiki/Jindai_moji

KARIMTO SCRIPT (TURKISH RUNES)

An ancient script that looks like Hangeul in some ways was found on a tombstone in Manchuria, China. Some Koreans believe that it is Karimto, a lost mythological script. However, professor Kijung Song from Seoul National University claims that the tombstone script is Turkish Runes, and a history blogger Mun-yeong Lee also argues in his book[7] that it is a series of symbolic script that the Huns[8] had used but it is unclear about the relevance between the Runes and Hangeul.

SANSKRIT

Sanskrit is an ancient language of India. As Buddhism started out from ancient India, the original Buddhist scriptures are written in Sanskrit. Since Buddhism was the state religion of Korea during the Silla Dynasty (57BC-935) and during the Goryeo Dynasty (918-1392), there is a likely relationship between Sanskrit and Korean. Juho Ahn, a professor at Sun-cheon-hyang University, argues that Hangeul was influenced by Sanskrit as a phonetic script for the idea of distinguishing consonants and vowels, and specifying the sounds made by the human vocal apparatus.[9] Su-seong Kim (known as Monk Shin-mi) was a Buddhist priest who is known to have participated in the creation of Hangeul. The recordings of a history book show that he was fluent in Sanskrit, Tibetan and Chinese in order to compare the original scriptures to the translated versions.

7 만들어진 한국사, Mun-yeong Lee, 2010
8 http://en.wikipedia.org/wiki/Huns
9 Hun Min Jeong Eum and Sanskrit, Juho Ahn, Taeseung Lee, 2009

In any case, Hangeul is the unique and complete alphabet invented by King Sejong in the 15th century and now being used as the official script in Korea. Its ease of use contributes to easy access to the Korean language.

2. HANGEUL OVERVIEW

Hangeul is a phonetic writing system.
Each symbol corresponds to a sound,
and each character is decoded from left-to-right
and then from top-to-bottom.

Hangeul is a phonetic writing system. Each symbol corresponds to a sound, for example 'ㅁ' is pronounced as 'm', 'ㅏ' as 'a' in 'father', and 'ㄴ' as 'n'. When you put the three together, you get '만', which is pronounced as 'man' in 'manga' (only pronouncing the underlined characters in the word).

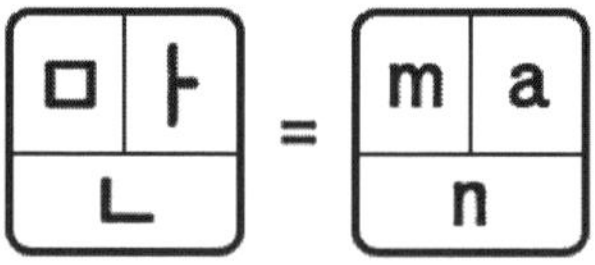

Each character is decoded from left-to-right and then from top-to-bottom. The vowel 'ㅣ' is pronounced as ' i ' in 'in', 'ㅗ' as 'o' in 'oh my', and 'ㅜ' as 'oo' in 'cool'. Thus, '민' is pronounced as 'minute', and '문' as 'moon'. Some characters are based on only two symbols, so '니' is pronounced as 'nifty', '나' as 'Tina', '노' as 'north', and '누' as 'noon'. Easy, isn't it?

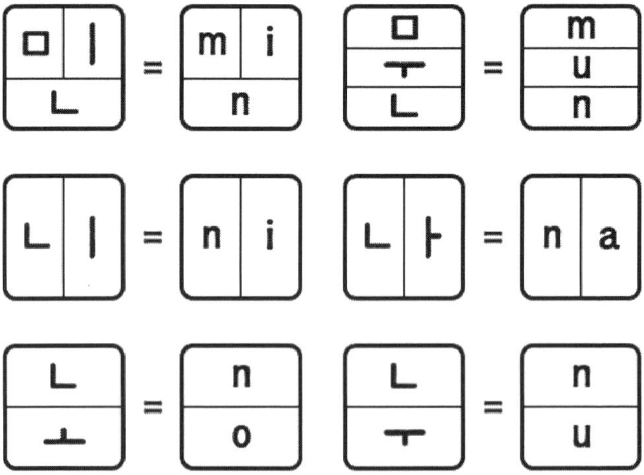

Well, not quite that easy. Otherwise it would not be so interesting to study. There are several rules that guide the composition of Hangeul characters.

The most important rule is that each Hangeul character must start with a consonant and must have one vowel. Based on this rule, '미' and '민' are valid Hangeul characters, but '口' or '|' is invalid or incomplete.

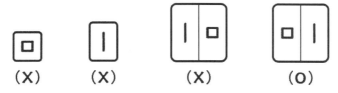

You may have observed that some vowels appear next to a consonant, while others appear below, such as the '|' in '미', and '⊤' in '무'. The reason is that some vowels are vertical while others are horizontal. (Later, we will encounter double vowels that are both vertical and horizontal.)

In Hangeul, the shape of consonants and vowels can also change based on the surrounding symbols, to make complete characters aesthetically pleasing. Here are a few examples:

만 곰 긴 미 동 다 른 리 읽

As you can see, the characters are roughly equal sized, the consonants and vowels expand and contract to fill the available space. A complication is that some consonants are pronounced differently depending on whether they appear in the beginning or at the end of a symbol. A good example is the consonant: 'O'. At the beginning of a character, it is silent, and at the end, it is pronounced as 'ng'. For example, '아' is pronounced as 'ah', and '잉' as 'ing'. Note that the symbol '잉' also is a good example for the rule we've seen earlier, that each symbol must begin with a consonant, where the initial 'O' is that consonant.

Congratulations! After just a few minutes, you can already read some Korean characters!

As for the character layout, Hangeul follows a basic rule : Each character must be composed in one of the nine patterns depicted below. The following nine characters each correspond to one pattern.

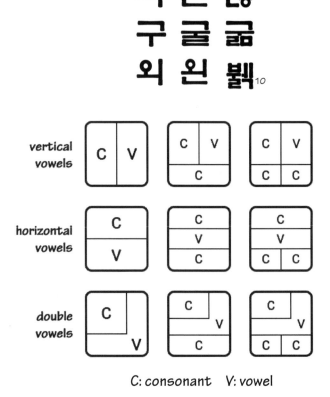

C: consonant   V: vowel

As you can see from this rule, each character must begin with a consonant. Moreover, each character can only have one vowel (although that vowel may be a double vowel as we will soon discover).

---

10 Interestingly, ' 뷁 ' is the only character that we are aware of for that last pattern. As it has a derogatory meaning, you'll be unlikely to encounter it (except in jokes).

We will now introduce all the consonants and vowels in detail. There are 20 basic letters[11] :

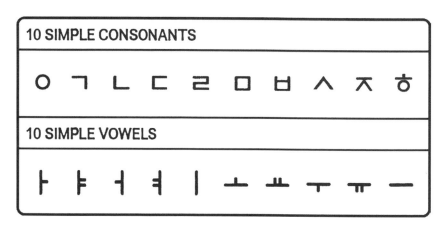

10 SIMPLE CONSONANTS
ㅇ ㄱ ㄴ ㄷ ㄹ ㅁ ㅂ ㅅ ㅈ ㅎ

10 SIMPLE VOWELS
ㅏ ㅑ ㅓ ㅕ ㅣ ㅗ ㅛ ㅜ ㅠ ㅡ

Although there are a total of 19 consonants and 21 vowels to learn, 9 consonants are simple variations of other consonants, and 11 vowels are simple variations of other vowels:

9 VARIATIONS OF CONSONANTS
ㅋ ㄲ ㅌ ㄸ ㅍ ㅃ ㅆ ㅊ ㅉ

11 VARIATIONS OF VOWELS
ㅐ ㅒ ㅔ ㅖ ㅢ ㅚ ㅘ ㅟ ㅝ ㅙ ㅞ

---

11 Although the basic consonants usually include 'ㅋ, ㅌ, ㅍ, ㅊ,' we attempt to minimize the learning effort by explaining 10 simple consonants first, and then derive 'ㅋ, ㅌ, ㅍ, ㅊ' from 'ㄱ, ㄷ, ㅂ, ㅈ' as variations. The correct lexicographic order is: 'ㄱ, ㄴ, ㄷ, ㄹ, ㅁ, ㅂ, ㅅ, ㅇ, ㅈ, ㅊ, ㅋ, ㅌ, ㅍ, ㅎ'.

The next page contains the table of consonants and vowels, listing the romanized Roman Alphabet letter, as well as a guide to its pronunciation. We are using the 'Revised Romanization of Korean'[12] with a few modifications on the consonants 'ㄱ, ㄲ, ㄸ, ㅃ' for better understandings on their actual pronunciation. Please note that the pronunciation of the individual romanized letters is quite different from how one would pronounce it in English. For example, the letter 'i' is pronounced in English as 'eye', but in the case of the romanized character it is pronounced as the 'i' in 'i̠nk'.

We will describe the sounds in detail in the following text, however, this table serves as an overview. The consonant table also categorizes the different pronunciations based on the location where sound is created (velar, coronal, bilabial, sibilant, or glottal, see diagram on Page26 to see a pictorial representation of these positions) and based on the sound itself (nasal, plosive & affricate, fricative, liquid). You don't need to worry about this terminology, as we will explain the detailed pronunciation later. However, it is interesting to note the systematic composition, where the different characters cover most of the combinations in the table. When the table notes two english consonants separated by a '/', for example 's / t' for 'ㅅ', the first character refers to the pronunciation if the character 'ㅅ' is a beginning consonant, and the second if it is an ending consonant. Some characters have alternate sounds as beginning characters, in which the table indicates the two options separated by a comma, for example 'ㄱ' is pronounced either as 'k' or 'g' as initial consonant, so the table lists 'k,g / g'.

12 'Revised Romanization of Korean' is the official Korean language romanization system in South Korea. It was developed by the National Academy of the Korean Language from 1995 and was released to the public on July 7, 2000, by South Korea's Ministry of Culture and Tourism in Proclamation No. 2000-8.

CONSONANTS

		VELAR	CORONAL	BILABIAL	SIBILANT	GLOTTAL
NASAL		O ·/ng	ㄴ n	ㅁ m		
PLOSIVE & AFFRICATE	PLAIN	ㄱ k,g/g	ㄷ d/t	ㅂ b/p	ㅈ j/t	
	ASPIRATED	ㅋ k	ㅌ t	ㅍ p	ㅊ ch/t	
	TENSE	ㄲ gg	ㄸ dd	ㅃ bb	ㅉ jj/t	
FRICATIVE	PLAIN				ㅅ s/t	ㅎ h/t
	TENSE				ㅆ ss/t	
LIQUID			ㄹ r/l			

VOWELS

	VERTICAL	HORIZONTAL	DOUBLE
LIGHT	ㅏ a ㅑ ya ㅐ ae ㅒ yae	ㅗ o ㅛ yo	ㅚ oe ㅘ wa ㅙ wae
NEUTRAL	ㅣ i	ㅡ eu	ㅢ ui
DEEP	ㅓ eo ㅕ yeo ㅔ e ㅖ ye	ㅜ u ㅠ yu	ㅟ wi ㅝ wo ㅞ we

Notice that there is a simplified version of the romanization table at the end of the book, so you can find it easily anytime you need.

In the following Chapter 3, we will learn the 19 consonants, and in Chapter 4 we will learn the 21 vowels. In Chapter 5, we will learn how to pronounce composed letters.

(!) TWO & TOOTH

이	KOREAN	이 (이빨)
two	ENGLISH	tooth
zwei	GERMAN	Zahn
deux	FRENCH	dent
dos	SPANISH	dento

Before we dive into the details, let's consider some interesting trivia. The Korean word '이' [ee] has three meanings: a family name, the word for tooth, and the number 2. Can you guess which family name it is? Yes, it is 'Lee' or 'Rhee', the 'L' or 'R' remain for historical reasons of how the Chinese character for the name was originally pronounced.

The other two meanings are the number 2 and a nickname for tooth. It is interesting that in several languages the word for number 2 and tooth are very similar, such as in English ('two' and 'tooth'), German ('zwei' and 'Zahn'), French ('deux' and 'dent'), Spanish ('dos' and 'dento'). Coincidence or not? Maybe a coincidence, as in Chinese or Japanese, this relationship does not hold.

3. CONSONANTS

Basic consonants, Intermediate consonants,
Aspirated consonants, and Double consonants

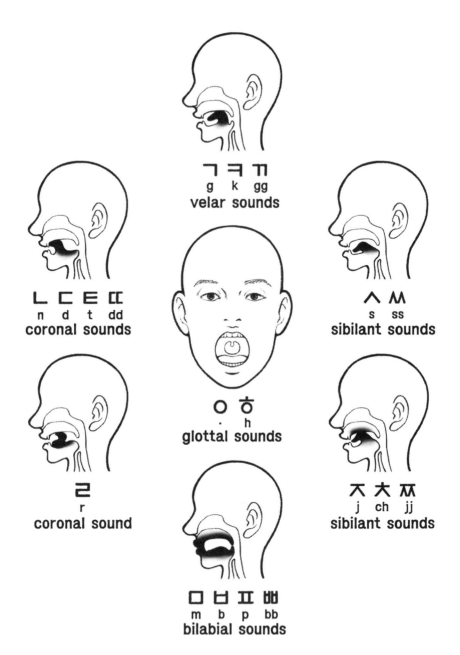

ㄱ ㅋ ㄲ
g k gg
velar sounds

ㄴ ㄷ ㅌ ㄸ
n d t dd
coronal sounds

ㅅ ㅆ
s ss
sibilant sounds

ㄹ
r
coronal sound

ㅇ ㅎ
· h
glottal sounds

ㅈ ㅊ ㅉ
j ch jj
sibilant sounds

ㅁ ㅂ ㅍ ㅃ
m b p bb
bilabial sounds

An interesting fact is that the shapes of these consonants were selected based on the shape of the mouth or tongue when voicing them! 'ㄱ', 'ㄴ' and 'ㄹ' mimic the shape of the tongue, while 'ㅁ' mimics the shape of the closed mouth, 'ㅅ' represents the air rushing out and 'ㅇ' shows the open throat.

26

(1) BASIC CONSONANTS

Let's first look at the five most common and basic consonants: 'ㄱ,ㄴ,ㅁ,ㅅ,ㅇ'.

The first consonant is 'ㄱ', called [gi-yeok]. At the beginning of a character it is pronounced as a weak 'k' or 'g'. The following two diagrams demonstrate a character that begins with 'ㄱ', the first shows a combination with a horizontal vowel and the second with a vertical vowel.

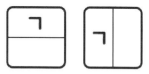

At the end of a character, it is pronounced as a barely audible 'g', which is pronounced by rapidly blocking the 'g' sound. The following diagram demonstrates the ending 'ㄱ'.

We will introduce each consonant and vowel with the following diagram:

ㄱ	go [k, g]	고기 [go-gi]: meat 김치 [kim-chi]: kimchi
기역 [gi-yeok]	bag [g]	목 [mog]: neck

In the diagram above, you can see the symbol and its name on the left hand column. The name of the symbol is written in Hangeul as well as in its Romanized form: ' 기역 ' [gi-yeok]. Please note that the square brackets indicate the romanized form, thus the pronunciation of the romanized text follows the rules described in the previous section and not standard English pronunciation.

The middle part of the diagram depicts the pronunciation, using English words and underlining the part of the word that sounds like the character when pronounced in standard English. The [g] with square brackets again indicates the romanized text. The top half indicates the pronunciation if the consonant is at the beginning of a character, the bottom half if it is at the end.

The right hand column provides examples utilizing the character, indicating different ways of writing it. With the diagram, you can also begin to learn some basic Korean words, as the Romanization and translation are provided as well.

The socond consonant is ' ㄴ ' called [ni-eun] ' 니은.' Fortunately, the consonant ' ㄴ ' is easy; it is simply pronounced as 'n' in English, whether it is positioned in the beginning or end of a character.

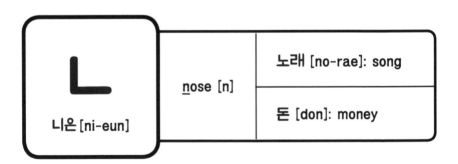

(!) CAUTION

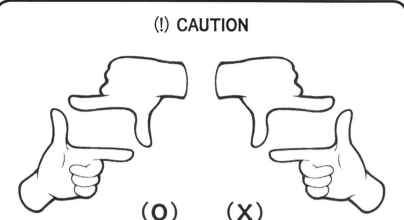

(O)   (X)

A potential source of confusion for Hangeul beginners is to differentiate whether 'ㄱ' and 'ㄴ' are correct, or whether it is 'ㄷ' and 'ㄴ'? An easy way to remember is that 'n' is written like a capital 'L', and 'g' is written by rotating 'L' by 180 degrees. As a memory aid, you can consider the alphabet sequence 'LMN', and remember 'L Means N.' So hopefully with this 'L' memory aid, it will be easy to note that 'ㄷ' and 'ㄴ' are invalid characters.

Another method for remembering is to realize that Hangeul writing is optimized for right-handed people: left-to-right and top-to-bottom. Even each individual character is written that way, as we will learn later. Thus, it is natural to write 'ㄱ' and 'ㄴ' in a single stroke, but if they were 'ㄷ' and 'ㄴ', the writing would require two strokes to write left-to-right and top-to-bottom.

The consonant '□' is easy as well. It is pronounced as 'm', as we learned in the previous chapter.

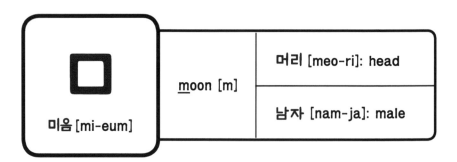

| □
미음 [mi-eum] | moon [m] | 머리 [meo-ri]: head |
| | | 남자 [nam-ja]: male |

The consonant '∧' is again interesting, because it is pronounced as a sharp 's' if it is in the beginning of a character, and as a 't' if it is at the end. Before the vowels 'ㅣ, ㅑ, ㅕ, ㅛ, ㅠ' it is pronounced as 'sh' though. We will soon learn these vowels.

Also as we will see later, this character exhibits some other interesting pronunciation issues depending on the surrounding consonants and vowels, which will keep us on our toes for some time. But for now, we'll keep things simple by considering pronunciation of a single character by itself.

| ∧
시옷 [shi-ot] | swing [s]
ship [sh] | 사자 [sa-ja]: lion |
| | cat [t] | 옷 [ot]: clothes |

The consonant 'O' has no sound at the beginning, but is pronounced 'ng' at the end of the character. This character can be considered to be like a silent 'k' in English, such as in the words 'know' or 'knot'. Recall the earlier rule that any character must start with a consonant? In the case when a word starts with a vowel, the voiceless 'O' is used to precede the vowel.

O 이응 [i-eung]	no sound	아이 [a-i]: child
	sing [ng]	공 [gong]: ball

EXAMPLES

나이 [na-i]: age

거미 [geo-mi]: spider

강 [gang]: river

시소 [shi-so]: seesaw

무 [mu]: daikon

모자 [mo-ja]: hat, cap

이모 [i-mo]: aunt

소리 [so-ri]: sound

나라 [na-ra]: country

소 [so]: cow

손 [son]: hand

솜 [som]: cotton

낫 [nat]: sickle

말 [mal]: horse

몸 [mom]: body

노인 [no-in]: old man

(2) INTERMEDIATE CONSONANTS

In this section, we will learn the consonants 'ㄷ,ㅂ,ㅈ,ㄹ.'

The consonant 'ㄷ' is pronounced as 'd' at the beginning, and as 't' at the end of a character. 'ㅂ' sounds like 'b' at the beginning, and as 'p' at the end, while 'ㅈ' is pronounced as 'j' if it is at the beginning and as 't' at the end.

ㄷ 디귿 [di-geut]	<u>d</u>esk [d]	다리 [da-ri]: leg, bridge
	ca<u>t</u> [t]	받침 [bat-chim]: prop

ㅂ 비읍 [bi-eup]	<u>b</u>ook [b]	바지 [ba-ji]: pants
	na<u>p</u> [p]	밥 [bap]: meal, rice

ㅈ 지읒 [ji-eut]	<u>j</u>acket [j]	자 [ja]: ruler
	ca<u>t</u> [t]	낮 [nat]: day

You may have noticed that several consonants we have seen so far sound like 't' if they are at the end of a character, namely: 'ㅅ, ㄷ, ㅈ.' It turns out that there are only 7 different final consonant sounds, which we will discuss in detail after we introduce all the consonants.

The last consonant we study in this section is 'ㄹ', which is pronounced as 'r' in 'ring', however, with a slight rolling 'r' sound. When at the end, however, it is pronounced as 'l'. This consonant may explain the frequent confusion between 'r' and 'l' by some Koreans. In any case, as we will see soon, the pronunciation of 'ㄹ' creates some intersting challenges.

ㄹ 리을 [ri-eul]	ribon [r]	루비 [ru-bi]: ruby
	camel [l]	술 [sul]: alcohol

EXAMPLES

집 [jip]: house

봄 [bom]: spring

두부 [du-bu]: tofu

돌 [dol]: stone

답 [dap]: answer

종 [jong]: bell

방 [bang]: room

부자 [bu-ja]: the rich

로마 [ro-ma]: Rome

비 [bi]: rain

(3) ASPIRATED CONSONANTS

The next five consonants we are going to learn are called "aspirated consonants", because they are voiced with a puff of air coming out of the mouth. The first is a new consonant, while the other four are variants of consonants we've already encountered.

The first consonant is 'ㅎ', which corresponds to 'h' in English if it is at the beginning, but is pronounced as 't' if it is at the end. If it is at the beginning, it is pronounced with a "puff of air".

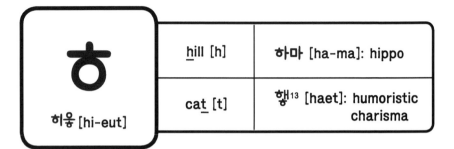

| ㅎ
 히읗 [hi-eut] | h<u>ill</u> [h] | 하마 [ha-ma]: hippo |
| | ca<u>t</u> [t] | 햏[13] [haet]: humoristic charisma |

The next four consonants are variants of other consonants we have already seen. If these new consonants are at the beginning, they are pronounced like the original one with the addition of a puff of air, however, if they are at the end, they are pronounced the same as the original consonant. The four are: 'ㅋ' derived from 'ㄱ', 'ㅌ' derived from 'ㄷ', 'ㅍ' derived from 'ㅂ', and 'ㅊ' derived from 'ㅈ'. 'ㅋ, ㅌ, ㅊ' just add another dash to the original consonant, while 'ㅍ' is written a bit differently.

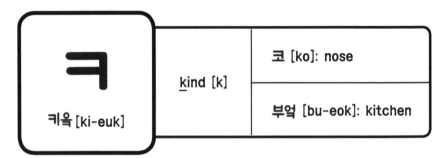

| ㅋ
 키읔 [ki-euk] | <u>k</u>ind [k] | 코 [ko]: nose |
| | | 부엌 [bu-eok]: kitchen |

---

13 햏 is a slang word used on the Internet since the year 2000.

|
ㅌ
티읕 [ti-eut] | <u>t</u>ea [t] | 통 [tong]: bucket |
| | | 밑 [mit]: the bottom |

|
ㅍ
피읖 [pi-eup] | <u>p</u>iano [p] | 파 [pa]: green onion |
| | | 잎 [ip]: leaf |

| **ㅊ**
치읓 [chi-eut] | <u>ch</u>air [ch] | 차 [cha]: car, tea |
| | ca<u>t</u> [t] | 숯 [sut]: charcoal |

EXAMPLES

하키 [ha-ki]: hockey

호두 [ho-du]: walnut

포도 [po-do]: grape

총 [chong]: gun

타조 [ta-jo]: ostrich

초 [cho]: candle

밭 [bat]: farming field

앞 [ap]: front

(4) DOUBLE CONSONANTS

Congratulations for getting this far! You have just a few more consonants to learn. The good news is that the remaining symbols are combinations of what you have already learned.

First, we learn 5 double consonants and they should look familiar: ' ㄲ , ㄸ , ㅃ , ㅆ , ㅉ .' They are called tensed consonants because if they occur at the beginning of the character, they are pronounced as the original consonants but in a more tense fashion. Similar to the aspirated consonants we have encountered above, tensed consonants are pronounced as the original consonants if they occur at the end of the character. (' ㄸ , ㅃ , ㅉ ' only exist as initial consonants.)

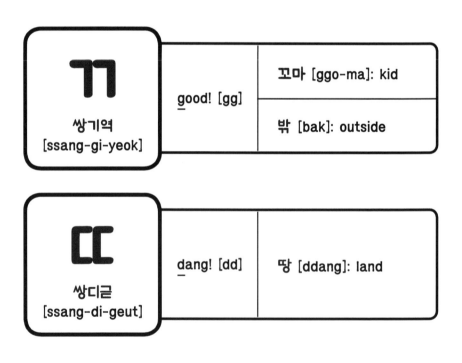

ㄲ 쌍기역 [ssang-gi-yeok]	<u>g</u>ood! [gg]	꼬마 [ggo-ma]: kid
		밖 [bak]: outside
ㄸ 쌍디귿 [ssang-di-geut]	<u>d</u>ang! [dd]	땅 [ddang]: land

쌍비읍
[ssang-bi-eup]

Audrey Hep<u>b</u>urn [bb]	빵 [bbang]: bread

쌍시옷
[ssang-shi-ot]

<u>s</u>ee! [ss]	쌍 [ssang]: double
ca<u>t</u> [t]	했다 [hat-da]: did

쌍디귿
[ssang-di-geut]

<u>d</u>ang! [dd]	땅 [ddang]: land

EXAMPLES

꿈 [ggum]: dream

꿀 [ggul]: honey

싸움 [ssa-um]: fight

딸 [ddal]: daughter

뽀뽀 [bbo-bbo]: kiss

또 [ddo]: again

쑥 [ssug]: mugwort

찜 [jjim]: steam

(!) EXTINCT & NEW SYMBOLS

There are extinct characters that existed in ancient Hangeul but disappeared because of lack of usage. Recent movements attempt to revive forgotten characters and even for creating new symbols for foreign language words to avoid homonyms.

For example, 'ㅇ' (no sound), 'ㆁ' and 'ㆆ' were each used in 15th century, but they were merged into 'ㅇ' since 16th century.

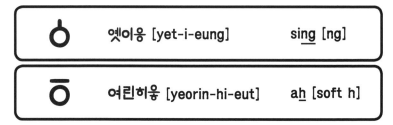

ㆁ	옛이응 [yet-i-eung]	si**ng** [ng]
ㆆ	여린히읗 [yeorin-hi-eut]	a**h** [soft h]

For 'ㅿ', there is an argument among scholars whether it was 'z' or 'y.' We marked it 'z' as it is more widely accepted.

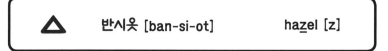

ㅿ	반시옷 [ban-si-ot]	ha**z**el [z]

'ㅸ', 'ㆄ', 'ㆆ' and 'ㅌ' are modified from 'ㅂ', 'ㅍ', 'ㄷ' and 'ㅌ', where the small 'ㅇ' on the bottom indicates a smoother pronunciation. For example in the case of 'ㆄ', the pronunciation is similar to 'ph' which is similar to an 'f' in English. There are also simplified candidates for these symbols suggested by several different scholars, so let's see which one gets picked. What do you prefer?

ㅸㅿㄴ	**v**ine [v]	ㆄㆅㅗ	**f**ish [f]
ㆆㄸㄲ	**th**e [th]	ㅌㅌㅁ	**th**in [th]

4. VOWELS

Basic Vowels, Y-Vowels, and Double Vowels

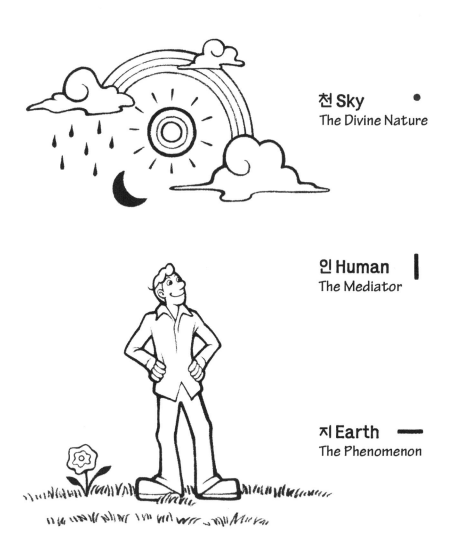

천 Sky •
The Divine Nature

인 Human |
The Mediator

지 Earth —
The Phenomenon

The vowels in Hangeul are patterned after the shapes of sky (·), earth (—) and human (|), so called Cheon Ji In (**천지인**). Any vowel in Hangeul is a combination of these three shapes. To simplify learning and usage, the Cheon Ji In humanistic philosophy would base vowels on familiar constructions.

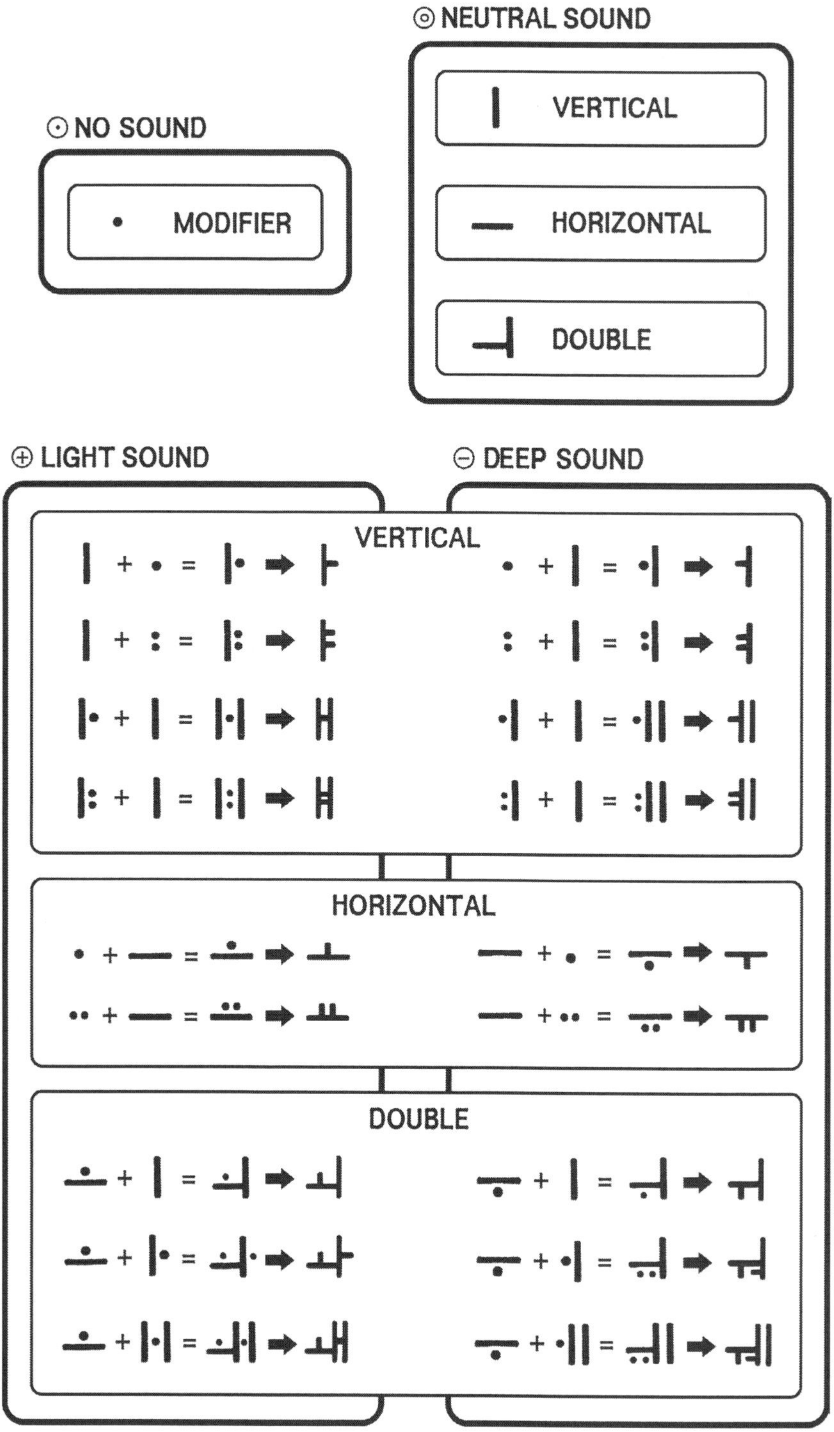

⊙ NO SOUND

•	MODIFIER

⊚ NEUTRAL SOUND

│	VERTICAL
—	HORIZONTAL
┙	DOUBLE

⊕ LIGHT SOUND

VERTICAL

│ + • = │• ➡ ┝

│ + ⦂ = │⦂ ➡ ┠

│• + │ = │•│ ➡ ╟

│⦂ + │ = │⦂│ ➡ ╠

HORIZONTAL

• + — = ∸ ➡ ┴

•• + — = ∺ ➡ ┵

DOUBLE

∸ + │ = ┵│ ➡ ┵

∸ + │• = ┵│• ➡ ┵

∸ + │•│ = ┵│•│ ➡ ┵

⊖ DEEP SOUND

VERTICAL

• + │ = •│ ➡ ┤

⦂ + │ = ⦂│ ➡ ┥

•│ + │ = •││ ➡ ┨

⦂│ + │ = ⦂││ ➡ ┫

HORIZONTAL

— + • = ⨪ ➡ ┬

— + •• = ⨪ ➡ ┰

DOUBLE

┬ + │ = ┬│ ➡ ┤

┬ + •│ = ┬•│ ➡ ┤

┬ + •││ = ┬•││ ➡ ┨

41

(1) BASIC VOWELS

Ready to learn some vowels? We will start with three vertical vowels: 'ㅏ', 'ㅓ', and 'ㅣ', followed by the three horizontal vowels 'ㅗ', 'ㅜ', and 'ㅡ'.

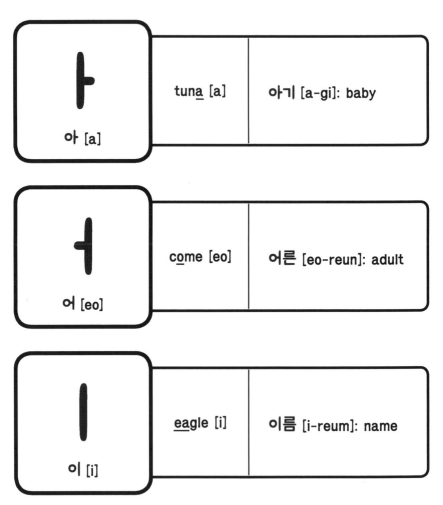

아 [a]	tun**a** [a]	아기 [a-gi]: baby
어 [eo]	c**o**me [eo]	어른 [eo-reun]: adult
이 [i]	**ea**gle [i]	이름 [i-reum]: name

The good news is that the vowels are always pronounced the same, in contrast to some of the troublesome consonants we saw before. The not-so-good news is that some of the vowels do not have exact equivalents in English, so prepare yourself for some long-term effort to get them right.

In fact, in our experience, ' ㅓ ' and ' ㅡ ' are the two trouble makers! ' ㅓ ' is pronounced somewhat like saying 'ah' and 'oh' at the same time, such as 'alright.' The challenge with ' ㅡ ' is that it also has no clear English equivalent; it is pronounced as 'm_e_rcy,' or the French word 'connaiss_eu_r,' or as the German Umlaut 'ö'.

When using ' ㅗ ', please be careful with the pronunciation, as it is pronounced more like you would say the initial syllable 'o' in 'm_o_ld', and not like 'ou' in 'm_ou_nd'.

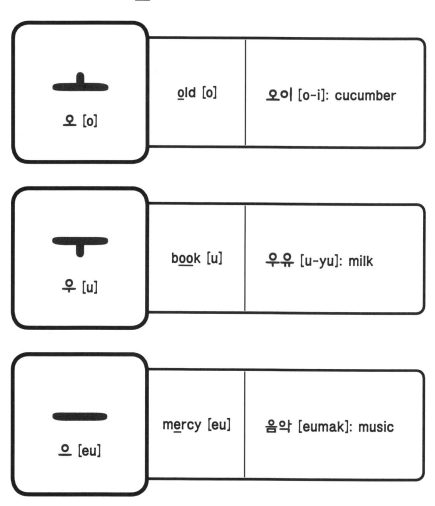

ㅗ 오 [o]	_o_ld [o]	오이 [o-i]: cucumber
ㅜ 우 [u]	b_oo_k [u]	우유 [u-yu]: milk
ㅡ 으 [eu]	m_e_rcy [eu]	음악 [eumak]: music

The next two vowels are '**ㅐ**' and '**ㅔ**'. While some younger Koreans simply pronounce both of them as 'e' in 'Eskimo', the correct pronunciation of '**ㅐ**' is a bit longer and contains a hint of 'a', such as the 'e' in 'hen'.

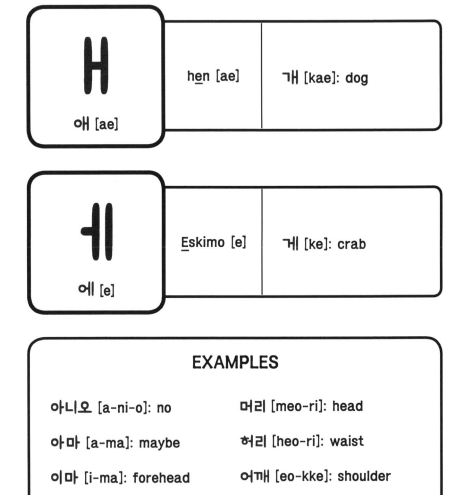

ㅐ 애 [ae]	h<u>e</u>n [ae]	개 [kae]: dog

ㅔ 에 [e]	<u>E</u>skimo [e]	게 [ke]: crab

EXAMPLES

아니오 [a-ni-o]: no

아마 [a-ma]: maybe

이마 [i-ma]: forehead

은 [eun]: silver

금 [geum]: gold

머리 [meo-ri]: head

허리 [heo-ri]: waist

어깨 [eo-kke]: shoulder

해 [hae]: sun

우주 [u-ju]: universe

(!) PATTERNS & SYMBOLS

It is interesting that Koreans like to use lots of lines and dots to make graphic patterns.

You can find many dots added on the left side of early Hangeul characters on Page 12. They were used until the end of 16th century to indicate high & low or long & short tones when pronouncing the characters.

Short & Low

Short & High

Long & High

You can also find the patterns made of black lines surrounding the circle in their national flag. These patterns each have names called Geon, Gam, Gon, Rhee (clockwise, starting at upper left). They are also known to have meanings of seasonal virtues.

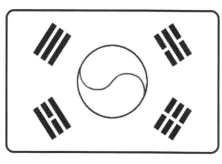

건 [Geon]
The Sky
Winter
(Wisdom)

감 [Gam]
The Sun
Spring
(Justice)

곤 [Gon]
The Earth
Summer
(Vitality)

리 [Rhee]
The Moon
Fall
(Fruition)

(2) Y-VOWELS

The next six vowels are called y-vowels and they are easy to learn, because they are written by adding one small stroke to a basic vowel and are pronounced by preceding the vowel with a 'y.' So 'ㅏ' becomes 'ㅑ', 'ㅓ' becomes 'ㅕ', 'ㅗ' becomes 'ㅛ', 'ㅜ' becomes 'ㅠ', 'ㅐ' becomes 'ㅒ', and 'ㅔ' becomes 'ㅖ'. The table below depicts the pronunciations.

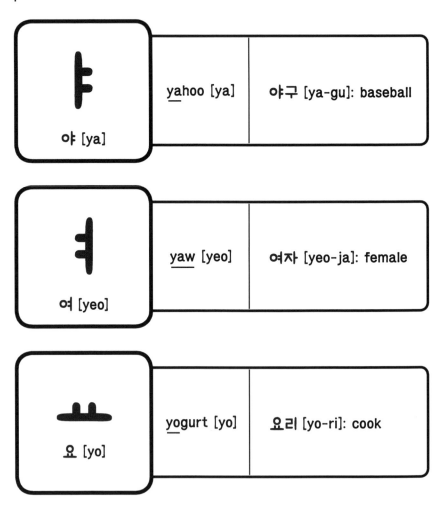

ㅑ 야 [ya]	yahoo [ya]	야구 [ya-gu]: baseball
ㅕ 여 [yeo]	yaw [yeo]	여자 [yeo-ja]: female
ㅛ 요 [yo]	yogurt [yo]	요리 [yo-ri]: cook

유 [yu] | you [yu] | 유아 [yu-a]: infant

애 [yae] | yale [yae] | 얘 [yae]: this fellow

예 [ye] | yes [ye] | 예술 [ye-sul]: art

EXAMPLES

여름 [yeo-reum]: summer   이야기 [i-ya-gi]: story

요술 [yo-sul]: magic   얘기 [yae-gi]: conversation

교실 [kyo-shil]: classroom   묘지 [myo-ji]: graveyard

유자 [yu-ja]: citron   예뻐 [ye-bbeo]: pretty

(3) DOUBLE VOWELS

The seven double vowels are combinations of one horizontal vowel with one vertical vowel: 'ㅚ, ㅘ, ㅙ, ㅝ, ㅟ, ㅞ, ㅢ'. The sound is a combination of the two vowels, where the horizontal vowel is voiced first but quickly followed by the vertical vowel. The table below describes their pronunciations.

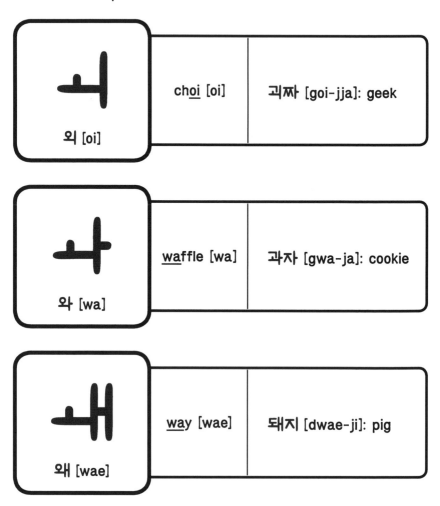

ㅚ [oi]	choi [oi]	괴짜 [goi-jja]: geek
ㅘ [wa]	waffle [wa]	과자 [gwa-ja]: cookie
ㅙ [wae]	way [wae]	돼지 [dwae-ji]: pig

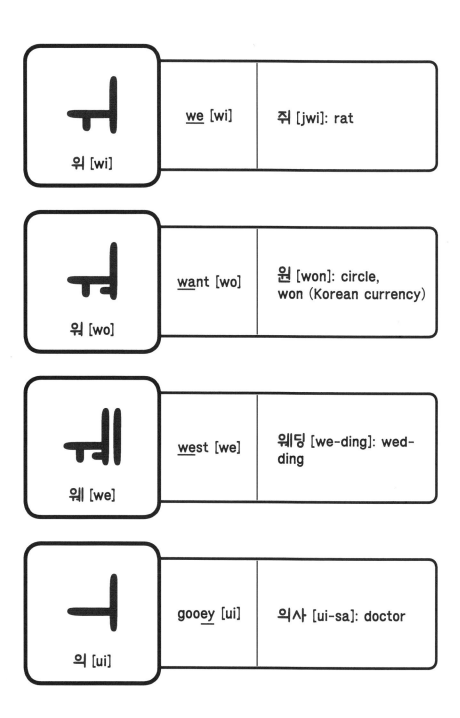

위 [wi]	<u>we</u> [wi]	쥐 [jwi]: rat
워 [wo]	<u>wa</u>nt [wo]	원 [won]: circle, won (Korean currency)
웨 [we]	<u>we</u>st [we]	웨딩 [we-ding]: wed-ding
의 [ui]	goo<u>ey</u> [ui]	의사 [ui-sa]: doctor

EXAMPLES

외모 [oi-mo]: appearance

의심 [ui-shim]: doubt

왕 [wang]: king

과일 [gwa-il]: fruit

샤워 [sha-wo]: shower

위기 [wi-gi]: crisis

왜 [wae]: why

월 [wol]: month

It may seem challenging to remember these seven combinations, but fortunately, we have devised a simple way to memorize them. The first three '긔, ㅓ, ㅟ' are the combination of 'ㅣ' with the three basic horizontal vowels 'ㅗ, ㅡ, ㅜ'. The next one 'ㅘ' is essentially the combination of 'ㅗ' rotated by 90 degrees to obtain 'ㅏ', as the figure below indicates. Then you can add one more vertical dash on the right hand side to obtain: 'ㅙ'. The final two are formed based on the same pattern. When you start with 'ㅜ' and rotate it by 90 degrees, you get 'ㅓ', and their combination yields 'ㅝ'. When you add one more vertical dash on the right hand side you get 'ㅞ'. Based on this rule, it is clear that you cannot combine 'ㅜ' with 'ㅏ' or 'ㅗ' with 'ㅓ'. The following diagram may help to visualize this concept.

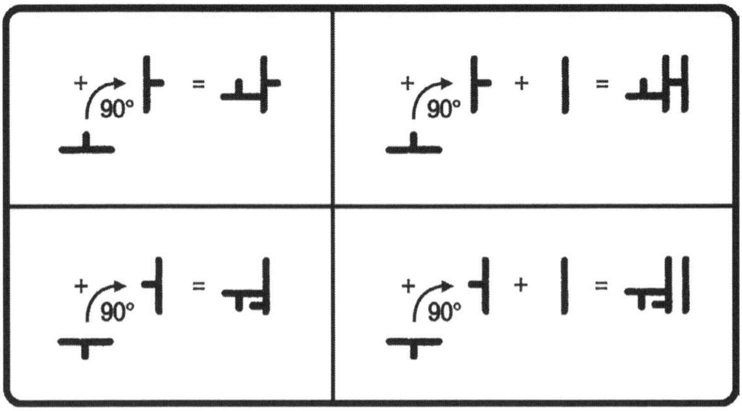

It turns out that this understanding can become very useful in reading the double vowels. Initially, reading double vowels can be confusing, because in many cases it is hard to discern the little lines to distinguish the characters. The reason why the short lines are often unclear or even omitted in text is because the ambiguous double vowel does not exist — hence, the actual vowel is the only legitimate combination. In the more advanced reading section, we will provide examples that illustrate this point.

Here is a simple rule on how to read double vowels:

1) If the vertical vowel is 'ㅣ':
  1.1) If the horizontal vowel is 'ㅗ' then 'ㅚ'
  1.2) If the horizontal vowel is 'ㅡ' then 'ㅢ'
  1.2) If the horizontal vowel is 'ㅜ' then 'ㅟ'
2) If the vertical vowel is 'ㅏ' then 'ㅘ'
3) If the vertical vowel is 'ㅐ' then 'ㅙ'
4) If the vertical vowel is 'ㅓ' then 'ㅝ'
5) If the vertical vowel is 'ㅔ' then 'ㅞ'

In essence, only if the vertical vowel is 'ㅣ' then you even need to look at the horizontal vowel. This now explains that for characters with double vowels that have one of the vertical vowel 'ㅏ, ㅐ, ㅓ, ㅔ', it is often hard to discern whether the horizontal vowel is 'ㅗ', 'ㅡ', or 'ㅜ.' The good news is that you don't need to even look because there is only one possible horizontal vowel combination.

So let's go through a small quiz to find the illegal vowels.

1. ①와 ②왜 ③위 ④유 ⑤웨

2. ①괘 ②뒈 ③뮈 ④류 ⑤희

ANSWER 1: ④ 2: ②

(!) LIGHT SOUNDS & DEEP SOUNDS

Two groups of vowel sounds describe different moods & emotions. We can see them in some of the following expressive sounds.

• Light Sound Vowels: ㅏ, ㅑ, ㅐ, ㅒ, ㅗ, ㅛ, ㅚ, ㅘ, ㅙ
These vowels make outgoing sounds, with air resonance mainly outside the mouth.

아 [ah]: found something out
오 [oh]: admires something
와 [wa]: surprized, excited
야호 [ya-ho]: excited
이랴 [ee-rya]: making a horse run

나나나 [nanana]: humming
라라라 [lalala]: singing
하하하 [hahaha]: laughing
으앗 [eu-at]: scared
앵앵 [aeng-aeng]: siren

· sample words in English: Ee-ha, Yay, Yikes, Ta-da

• Deep Sound Vowels: ㅓ, ㅕ, ㅔ, ㅖ, ㅜ, ㅠ, ㅓ, ㅝ, ㅞ
These vowels make inner sounds with air resonance mainly on the inner side of the mouth.

어 [eoh]: unclear about something
우 [ooh]: teasing someone
워 [wo]: making a horse stop
엉엉엉 [eong-eong-eong]: crying
쿡쿡 [kukkuk]: secretly laughing

얼쑤 [eol-su]: grooving
후 [hoo]: regrets
휘유 [hwi-yu]: relieved
에휴 [e-hyu]: disappointed
에잇 [e-it]: squeezing feast

· sample words in English: Uh, Umm, Huh, Boo

• Mixture of light & deep sound emphasizes expressions.

우와 [u-wa]: very impressed
우오오 [u-o-o]: very impressed

우왕 [u-wang]: very excited
어야 [eo-ya]: far away

· sample words in English: Hooray, Wow, Ouch, Ulala

5. PRONUNCIATIONS OF COMBINED CHARACTERS

The pronunciation of a consonant can be affected by consonants and vowels that follow in the subsequent character. Thus, the correct pronunciation turns out to be complex in some cases.

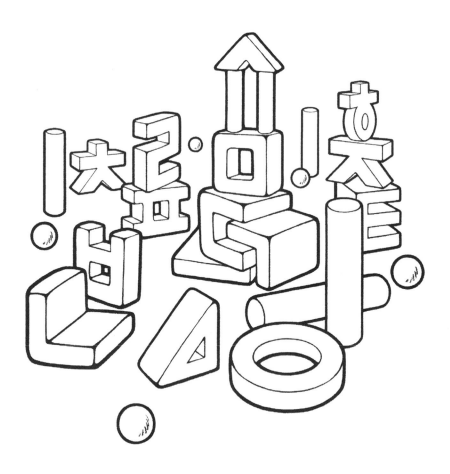

So far, we have only considered the pronunciation of single Hangeul characters. Unfortunately, the pronunciation of a consonant can be affected by consonants and vowels that follow in the subsequent character. Thus, the correct pronunciation turns out to be complex in some cases. We suggest that you learn this as you advance in your Korean studies, and that you keep returning to this chapter over time. So for now, simply read through this chapter and appreciate the rules with the understanding that you will internalize them over time.

(1) BASIC RULES

Rule 1.1

When a final consonant is followed by an initial consonant 'O' in the following syllable, that consonant is carried over to the following syllable to function as its initial consonant in pronunciation. When the final consonant is a double consonant, only the last consonant will be carried over. For instance, '연어 [yeon-eo]: salmon' is read as '여너 [yeo-neo].' The following diagram depicts this rule, where the number 1 stands for any consonant, and the second character starts with the silent consonant 'O' (and thus we also say that it starts with a vowel).

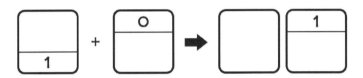

This transformation only occurs for pronunciation purposes, the writing does not change. We indicate this transformation with the '➡' symbol. Here are some examples:

EXAMPLES

먹어 ➡ 머거 [meo-geo]: eat, help yourself

맞아 ➡ 마자 [ma-ja]: you're right

입어 ➡ 이버 [i-beo]: put on, get dressed

한국어 ➡ 한구거 [han-gu-geo]: Korean language

했어 ➡ 해써 [hae-sseo]: did

This rule changes the pronunciation considerably. Consider the word for 'this': ' 이곳 ' pronounced as [i-got]. As we have learnt, the consonant '人' at the end is pronounced as 't', but it is pronounced as 's' in the beginning. So if we add the suffix ' 은 ', we get '이곳은' which becomes '이고슨' after applying **Rule1** and is thus pronounced as 'i-go-seun.' Hence, the 't' at the end is converted into 's' just by adding a suffix! This can be quite confusing at first, because suffixes get often added in Korean which can affect pronunciation.

This rule also applies to double final consonants, but there are some irregularities. Consider the table and diagram below. The table has three rows, corresponding to the numbers 1, 2, and 3 in the diagram. The final consonants in row 1 get separated and the later consonant replaces the silent consonant ' O ' of the second character. Note again that this only happens for pronunciation, not for writing purposes. In the table, we indicate the three irregular cases, where the final '人' seems to be the trouble maker. In case of ' ᄂᄒ ' and ' ᄚ ', 'ᄒ' just disappears (see **Rule5** on Page 66 for more details).

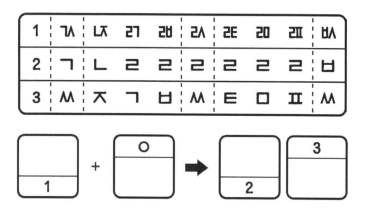

1	ᆪ	ᆬ	ᆰ	ᆲ	ᆳ	ᆴ	ᆱ	ᆵ	ᆹ
2	ㄱ	ㄴ	ㄹ	ㄹ	ㄹ	ㄹ	ㄹ	ㄹ	ㅂ
3	ㅆ	ㅈ	ㄱ	ㅂ	ㅆ	ㅌ	ㅁ	ㅍ	ㅆ

EXAMPLES

읊어 ➡ 을퍼 [eul-peo]: to recite

없어 ➡ 업써 [eop-sseo]: not here, does not exist

Rule 1.2

Exceptionally when a consonant ending in '**ㄷ**' or '**ㅌ**' is followed by a vowel '**ㅣ**', the '**ㄷ**' or '**ㅌ**' are pronounced '**ㅈ**' or '**ㅊ**', which is called Palatalization.

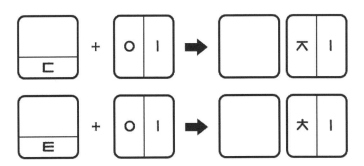

EXAMPLES

미닫이 ➡ 미다지 [mi-da-ji]: sliding door

같이 ➡ 가치 [ga-chi]: together, like (preposition)

맏이 ➡ 마지 [ma-ji]: the oldest one among siblings

샅샅이 ➡ 삳사치 [sat-sa-chi]: every nook and cranny

(2) SYLLABLE-FINAL CLOSURE

All final consonants are pronounced as one of seven ending sounds: ㅇ,ㄱ,ㄴ,ㄷ,ㄹ,ㅁ,ㅂ. Unfortunately, double final consonants cause some irregularity.

Rule 2.1

Only the first consonant of the double final consonant is pronounced. This is the case for: ㄳ,ㄵ,ㄶ,ㄽ,ㄾ,ㅀ,ㅄ.

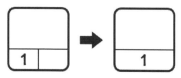

EXAMPLES

몫 ➡ 목 [mog]: portion   값 ➡ 갑 [gap]: price

Rule 2.2

Only the second consonant of the double final consonant is pronounced. This is the case for: ㄻ, ㄿ. A simple way to memorize these two is to remember ㄹ PM (ㄹ Prime Minister).

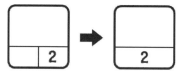

EXAMPLES

삶 ➡ 삼 [sam]: life   읊다 ➡ 읍다 [eup-da]: recite

ㄺ and ㄼ can occur in either case: in some cases, the former consonant is pronounced, and in other cases the latter. For example: '밟다 ➡ 밥다 [bap-da]: step on' which follows **Rule 2.2**, but commonly ㄼ follows **Rule 2.1**, as in '여덟 ➡ 여덜 [yeo-deol]: eight.'

The following table shows all possible final consonants and their pronunciation. This table is very useful and we encourage memorization.

FINAL CONSONANTS	PRONUNCIATION
ㅇ	[ng]
ㄱ ㅋ ㄲ ㄳ (ㄺ)	[g]
ㄴ ㄵ ㄶ	[n]
ㄷ ㅌ ㅅ ㅆ ㅈ ㅊ ㅎ	[t]
ㄹ (ㄼ) ㄽ ㄾ ㅀ (ㄺ)	[l]
ㅁ ㄻ	[m]
ㅂ ㅍ ㄿ ㅄ (ㄼ)	[p]

EXAMPLES

밖 ➡ 박 [bag]: outside   낫 ➡ 낟 [nat]: sickle

부엌 ➡ 부억 [bu-eog]: kitchen   낮 ➡ 낟 [nat]: day, noon

돛대 ➡ 돋대 [dot-dae]: mast   낯 ➡ 낟 [nat]: face, honor

숲 ➡ 숩 [sup]: forest   낱 ➡ 낟 [nat]: each

(3) ASSIMILATION

The assimilation rule assimilates (i.e., makes similar) consecutive consonants. The intuition is that Koreans do not like to say a sequence of consonants that are not pronounced harmoniously, such as 'ㅅ, ㄹ, ㄱ,' because that may make a knot in one's tongue. Joking aside, you can think of it as the "lazy tongue rule," where consonants change their pronunciation based on neighboring consonants in order to keep the sound enjoyable and the tongue relaxed.

Rule 3.1

The first case of consonant assimilation is called Nasalization, where a final 'ㄱ' sound is replaced with 'ㅇ' (i.e., 'ng' because 'ㅇ' is at the end) when a nasal sound follows, such as 'ㄴ' or 'ㅁ'.

$$1 : ㄱ, ㅋ, ㄲ, ㄳ, ㄺ \rightarrow ㅇ$$

	L,ㅁ		L,ㅁ
1	+	→	ㅇ

EXAMPLES

부엌문 → 부엉문 [bu-eong-mun]: kitchen door

한국말 → 한궁말 [han-gung-mal]: Korean language

닭날개 → 당날개 [dang-nal-gae]: chicken wing

Rule 3.2

In the case of a final '**ㄷ**' sound, it is replaced (or 'nasalized' if that word exists) into '**ㄴ**' if it comes before '**ㄴ**' or '**ㅁ**'.

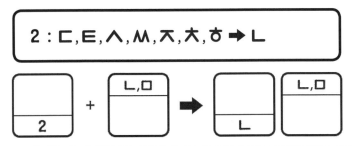

EXAMPLES

갔네 ➡ 간네 [gan-ne]: be gone

첫눈 ➡ 천눈 [cheon-nun]: the first sight, the first snow

맞는말 ➡ 만는말 [man-neun-mal]: true word

Rule 3.3

The third case of nasalization is where the final consonant is '**ㅂ**', which becomes '**ㅁ**'.

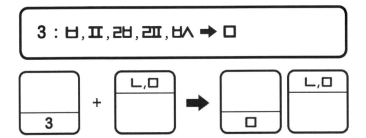

EXAMPLES

앞머리 ➡ 암머리 [am-meo-ri]: bangs (fore hair)

십만 ➡ 심만 [sim-man]: hundred thousand

합니다 ➡ 함니다 [ham-ni-da]: do

Rule 3.4

If final consonants are '**O**' or '**ㅁ**' in front of '**ㄹ**', '**ㄹ**' becomes '**ㄴ**'.

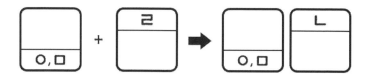

EXAMPLES

담력 ➡ 담녁 [dam-nyuk]: courage

종료 ➡ 종뇨 [jong-nyo]: end

Rule 3.5

In this case, both of two consonants which are adjoined change other consonants. We call this 'mutual assimilation'.

> 1 : ㄱ, ㅋ, ㄲ, ㄳ, ㄺ ➡ O
> 2 : ㄷ, ㅌ, ㅅ, ㅆ, ㅈ, ㅊ, ㅎ ➡ ㄴ
> 3 : ㅂ, ㅍ, ㄼ, ㄿ, ㅄ ➡ ㅁ

EXAMPLES

십리 ➡ 심니 [sim-ni]: 10리 (3.93km)

독립 ➡ 동닙 [dong-nip]: independence

대학로 ➡ 대항노 [dae-hang-no]: campus road

폭리 ➡ 퐁니 [pong-ni]: excessive profits

Rule 3.6

The next rule is called "Voicing," where the combination of ' ㄴ ' followed by ' ㄹ ' or ' ㄹ ' followed by ' ㄴ ' becomes ' ㄹ ' followed by ' ㄹ '.

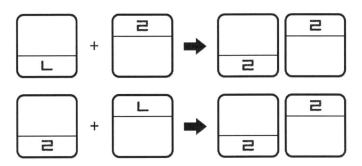

EXAMPLES

논리 ➡ 놀리 [nol-li]: logic

난리 ➡ 날리 [nal-li]: fuss

난로 ➡ 날로 [nal-lo]: heater, stove

연로 ➡ 열로 [yeol-lo]: old age

칼날 ➡ 칼랄 [kal-lal]: the edge of a knife

(!) CAUTION

Note that two consecutive ' ㄹ ' consonants are always pronounced as ' l ,' even if the second consonant in isolation would be pronounced as ' r ,' because it is before a vowel.

(4) COALESCENCE

Rule 4

In this rule, the consonant 'ㅎ' transforms the neighboring consonant into an aspirated consonant. The following table describes the two cases.

Rule 4.1

In the first case, 'ㅎ' precedes the next consonant.

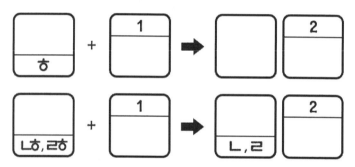

EXAMPLES

좋다 ➡ 조타 [jo-ta]: good, fine, like

낳다 ➡ 나타 [na-ta]: bear, give a birth

많다 ➡ 만타 [man-ta]: a lot, plenty

옳지 ➡ 올치 [ol-chi]: right, correct

앓다 ➡ 알타 [al-ta]: sick, not feeling well

잃고 ➡ 일코 [il-ko]: loose( ) + and(~)

Rule 4.2

In the second case, '**ㅎ**' follows the consonant.

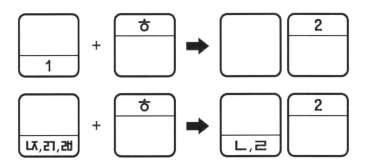

EXAMPLES

낙하산 ➡ 나카산 [na-ka-san]: parachute

잡히다 ➡ 자피다 [ja-pi-da]: get caught

앉히다 ➡ 안치다 [an-chi-da]: let sit

(5) DELETION

Rule 5

The consonant 'ㅎ' is not pronounced between voiced sounds.

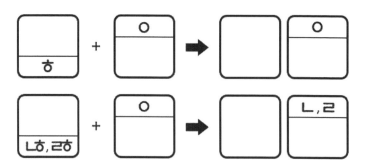

EXAMPLES

낳아 ➡ 나아 [na-a]: to give birth

놓아 ➡ 노아 [no-a]: put away, let go

많이 ➡ 만이 ➡ 마니 [ma-ni]: many, much, plenty

싫어 ➡ 실어 ➡ 시러 [si-reo]: dislike

The following table depicts the pronunciation rules depending on the final consonant (vertical) and the initial consonant (horizontal). The white area indicates where no special rule applies.

Phonological rule table (NEXT → columns, PREV ↓ rows)

PREV ↓ \ NEXT →	ㅇ	ㄱ	ㄴ	ㄷ	ㄹ	ㅁ	ㅈ	ㅎ	ETC.
ㅇ					R 3.4				
ㄱ ㅋ ㄲ,ㄳ,ㄺ	R 1.1		R 3.1		R 3.5	R 3.1		R 4.2	
ㄴ ㄵ					R 3.6				
ㄷ ㅌ ㅅ ㅆ ㅈ ㅊ	R 1.2 / R 1.1		R 3.2		R 3.5	R 3.2		R 4.2	no change
ㅎ ㄶ,ㅀ	R 5	R 4.1	R 4.1				R 4.1		
ㄹ ㄹㅅ,ㄹㅌ,ㄹㅁ			R 3.6						
ㅁ	R 1.1				R 3.4				
ㅂ ㅍ ㄼ,ㄿ,ㅄ			R 3.3		R 3.5	R 3.3		R 4.2	

ETC. : ㅂ , ㅅ , ㅋ , ㅌ , ㅍ , ㅊ , ㄲ , ㄸ , ㅃ , ㅆ , ㅉ

67

(!) MUCH MANY MORE

There are some Korean words that sound very similar to the words in English. For example, these three words sound very much like 'much', 'many', and 'more'.

무척 [mu-cheok]: very, extremely
많이 [ma-ni]: many, much, plenty
모아 [mo-a]: gather, collect

The word '많이' is an adjective that means 'many' as the way it is pronounced! It is derived from its original form, '많다.' '무척' is an adverb that means 'very', and '모아' is a verb that means 'gather'.

Even though the two words '무척' and '모아' have slightly different meanings from 'much' and 'more', it is interesting that somehow they are all related to the meanings of expansion. If you think of this rhyme, it will be easier to memorize the words:

"Much Many More, 무척 많이 모아, Very Much Gather"

6. PRACTICE

Let's practice!

(1) HANGEUL WRITING

The fundamental rule for writing Hangeul is that you write a character left-to-right and top-to-bottom. However, each consonant or vowel symbol is completed one-by-one: you don't start writing another consonant or vowel unless you completed the previous consonant or vowel. To really impress your Korean friends, you will need to write Hangeul using the correct stroke order, which we will study in this section. Simply follow the exercises, and you are a big step closer in becoming a Hangeul-master.

The following figure shows how we're going to indicate how to write a character. The arrows show the direction of the stroke and the numbers show the sequence. Just remember: left-to-right and top-to-bottom. The rest is intuitive.

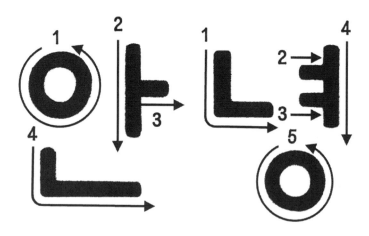

BASIC CONSONANTS

ㄱ	ㄱ	ㄱ				
ㄱ|역[ki-yeok]						
ㄴ	ㄴ	ㄴ				
ㄴ|은[ni-eun]						
ㅁ	ㅁ	ㅁ				
ㅁ|음[mi-eum]						
ㅅ	ㅅ	ㅅ				
ㅅ|웃[shi-ot]						
ㅇ	ㅇ	ㅇ				
ㅇ|웅[i-eung]						

INTERMEDIATE CONSONANTS

ㄷ	ㄷ	ㄷ				
ㄷ|귿[di-geot]						
ㄹ	ㄹ	ㄹ				
ㄹ|을[ri-eul]						
ㅂ	ㅂ	ㅂ				
ㅂ|읍[bi-eup]						
ㅈ	ㅈ	ㅈ				
ㅈ|웆[ji-eut]						
ㅎ	ㅎ	ㅎ				
ㅎ|읗[hi-eut]						

ASPIRATED CONSONANTS

키읔[ki-eok]						
티읕[ti-eut]						
피읖[pi-eup]						
치읓[chi-eut]						
☺						

VERTICAL VOWELS

아 [a]						
야 [ya]						
어 [eo]						
여 [yeo]						
이 [i]						

72

HORIZONTAL VOWELS

오 [o]						
요 [yo]						
우 [u]						
유 [yu]						
으 [eu]						

VERTICAL VOWELS 2

애 [ae]						
얘 [yae]						
에 [e]						
예 [ye]						

73

DOUBLE VOWELS

외 [oi]					
와 [wa]					
왜 [wae]					
위 [wi]					
워 [wo]					
웨 [we]					
의 [ui]					

74

(2) KOREAN WORDS IN HANGEUL

Now we are going to practice writing some Korean words.

[ko-kki-ri] elephant			
[tong] bucket			
[so-geum] salt			
[hu-chu] pepper			
[so-na-mu] pine tree			
[hae] sun			
[dal] moon			
[pyo-beom] leopard			
[ye-ui] politeness			
[honin] marriage			

노래 [no-rae] song	노래		
동화 [dong-hwa] fairytale	동화		
당근 [dang-geun] carrot	당근		
만두 [man-du] dumpling	만두		
멍멍 [meong-meong] bark	멍멍		
야옹 [yaong] meow	야옹		
당나귀 [dang-na-gui] donkey	당나귀		
잠 [jam] sleep	잠		
치마 [chi-ma] skirt	치마		
비둘기 [bi-dul-gi] pigeon	비둘기		

Doing great!

(3) ENGLISH WORDS IN HANGEUL

Now, we're going to try something unconventional: we're going to write English text with Hangeul characters. So instead of writing "Hello," we're going to write " 헬로 ."

Can you guess what this means:

" 하우 아 유 두잉 ? "

Yes indeed, it's "How are you doing?" The sound is a bit different due to the fact that Hangeul cannot encode all English sounds. Similarly, English writing cannot express Korean pronunciation either. Before we start, let's have some more examples to practice.

EXAMPLES

땡큐! ➡ Thank you!

아임 쏘리 ➡ I'm sorry.

커피 ➡ coffee

바이 바이~ ➡ bye bye~

와우 ➡ wow

스마트폰 ➡ smartphone

고릴라 ➡ gorilla

please ➡ 플리즈

Give me that! ➡ 깁 미 댇!

bunny ➡ 버니

puppy ➡ 퍼피

marshmallow ➡ 마시멜로우

chocolate ➡ 초콜렛

cozy ➡ 코지

The text in the yellow box is a paragraph in English written in Hangeul, and below is the same text written in alphabet. Feel free to read this many times over, until the decoding becomes natural.

언포츄너틀리, 코리안 더즈 낫 해브 더 컨서넌트 'f'. 쏘, 웬 유 트라이 투 라잇 잇 유 니드 투 유즈 'ㅍ'. 앤 웬 데어 이즈 언 'r' 앳 디 엔드 어브 더 워드, 유 캔 저스트 델릿 더 사운드 라더 덴 푸팅 'ㄹ' 앳 더 버텀 비커즈 잇 윌 비 프로나운스드 애즈 'l'. 얼소, 컨세큐티브 컨서넌츠 아 하드 투 라잇, 쏘 인 코리안 데이 겟 스플릿 업 위드 'ㅡ' 쏘 댓 더 컨서넌츠 어피어 인 더 비기닝 어브 더 캐릭터 앤드 아 더스 프라펄리 보이스, 라익 인 더 워드 '프로퍼' (proper). 이니셜리 잇 캔 비 어 빗 트릭키 투 리드 디스, 벗 에프터 어 와일 유 윌 겟 유즈드 투 잇 앤드 나우 유 캔 라잇 얼모스트 에니띵 인 어 뉴 알파벳!

Unfortunately, Korean does not have the consonant 'f'. So, when you try to write it you need to use 'ㅍ'. And when there is an 'r' at the end of the word, you can just delete the sound rather then putting 'ㄹ' at the bottom because it will be pronounced as 'l'. Also, consecutive consonants are hard to write, so in Korean they get split up with 'ㅡ' so that the consonants appear in the beginning of the character and are thus properly voice, like in the word '프로퍼' (proper). Initially it can be a bit tricky to read this, but after a while you will get used to it and now you can write almost anything in a new alphabet!

7. ADVANCED SKILLS

Various ways of Reading & Writing Hangeul

After studying this section, you probably think you're ready to embark to Seoul and read Hangeul like a native. Not so quickly though... 한글 is not quite THAT easy!

Fortunately, with a little bit of additional information, you can readily decode the majority of signs that you see, trusting that even Koreans will have trouble with the hand written signs that you cannot read.

The secret to reading Hangeul handwriting and difficult-to-read signs is called "constraint solving" to eliminate impossible choices: the Hangeul writing rules create constraints that will eliminate all ambiguities, leaving you with only a single character that is possible. The more advanced your Hangeul reading, the more automated this process becomes.

In the beginning, however, it can easily take quite a bit of time to go through all the possibilities until you get to the correct character. It's fun, so just look at it as a kind of puzzle. When you're on a subway ride in Seoul, there are plenty of challenging characters to decode to give you a fun ride! OK, let's get started with Hangeul- puzzle-solving, ahem... Hangeul reading.

The first complication comes from the fact that there are several ways to write the consonant and vowel symbols. The shape can also depend on the surrounding characters, for exmaple, the ' ㄱ ' character can look quite different in front of a vertical vowel, for example in ' 가 ' as the vertical line is slanted towards the left in some fonts. Presumably the slant makes the character more attractive in that case, although it can be confusing for beginners to identify the character.

The following table shows alternate ways to write the different consonant and vowel symbols.

ALTERNATE WAYS TO WRITE CONSONANT SYMBOLS

ㅇ	ㅇ	ㅇ	ㅇ	ㅇ	ㅇ
ㄱ	ㄱ	ㄱ	ㄱ	ㄱ	ㄱ
ㅋ	ㅋ	ㅋ	ㅋ	ㅋ	ㅋ
ㄲ	ㄲ	ㄲ	ㄲ	ㄲ	ㄲ
ㄴ	ㄴ	ㄴ	ㄴ	ㄴ	ㄴ
ㄷ	ㄷ	ㄷ	ㄷ	ㄷ	ㄷ
ㄸ	ㄸ	ㄸ	ㄸ	ㄸ	ㄸ
ㅌ	ㅌ	ㅌ	ㅌ	ㅌ	ㅌ
ㄹ	ㄹ	ㄹ	ㄹ	ㄹ	ㄹ
ㅁ	ㅁ	ㅁ	ㅁ	ㅁ	ㅁ
ㅂ	ㅂ	ㅂ	ㅂ	ㅂ	ㅂ
ㅍ	ㅍ	ㅍ	ㅍ	ㅍ	ㅍ
ㅃ	ㅃ	ㅃ	ㅃ	ㅃ	ㅃ
ㅅ	ㅅ	ㅅ	ㅅ	ㅅ	ㅅ
ㅆ	ㅆ	ㅆ	ㅆ	ㅆ	ㅆ
ㅈ	ㅈ	ㅈ	ㅈ	ㅈ	ㅈ
ㅊ	ㅊ	ㅊ	ㅊ	ㅊ	ㅊ
ㅉ	ㅉ	ㅉ	ㅉ	ㅉ	ㅉ
ㅎ	ㅎ	ㅎ	ㅎ	ㅎ	ㅎ

ALTERNATE WAYS TO WRITE VOWEL SYMBOLS

ㅏ	ㅏ	ㅓ	ㅏ	ㅏ	
ㅑ	ㅑ	ㅕ	ㅑ	ㅑ	
ㅓ	ㅓ	ㅓ	ㅓ	ㅓ	
ㅕ	ㅕ	ㅕ	ㅕ	ㅕ	
ㅣ	ㅣ	ㅣ	ㅣ	ㅣ	
ㅗ	ㅗ	ㅗ	ㅗ	ㅗ	
ㅛ	ㅛ	ㅛ	ㅛ	ㅛ	
ㅜ	ㅜ	ㅜ	ㅜ	ㅜ	
ㅠ	ㅠ	ㅠ	ㅠ	ㅠ	
ㅡ	ㅡ	ㅡ	ㅡ	ㅡ	
ㅐ	ㅐ	ㅐ	ㅐ	ㅐ	
ㅒ	ㅒ	ㅒ	ㅒ	ㅒ	
ㅔ	ㅔ	ㅔ	ㅔ	ㅔ	
ㅖ	ㅖ	ㅖ	ㅖ	ㅖ	
ㅚ	ㅚ	ㅚ	ㅚ	ㅚ	
ㅘ	ㅘ	ㅘ	ㅘ	ㅘ	
ㅙ	ㅙ	ㅙ	ㅙ	ㅙ	
ㅟ	ㅟ	ㅟ	ㅟ	ㅟ	
ㅝ	ㅝ	ㅝ	ㅝ	ㅝ	
ㅞ	ㅞ	ㅞ	ㅞ	ㅞ	
ㅢ	ㅢ	ㅢ	ㅢ	ㅢ	

EXAMPLES

BASIC	FORMAL	NOBLE	CASUAL	ARTISTIC
고기 (Meat)	고기	고기	고기	고기
노래 (Song)	노래	노래	노래	노래
돈 (Money)	돈	돈	돈	돈
라면 (Ramen)	라면	라면	라면	라면
마술 (Magic)	마술	마술	마술	마술
바보 (Fool)	바보	바보	바보	바보
사랑 (Love)	사랑	사랑	사랑	사랑
우유 (Milk)	우유	우유	우유	우유
정원 (Garden)	정원	정원	정원	정원
친구 (Friend)	친구	친구	친구	친구
쾅 (Thump)	쾅	쾅	쾅	쾅
턱 (Chin)	턱	턱	턱	턱
포도 (Grape)	포도	포도	포도	포도
휴가 (Vacation)	휴가	휴가	휴가	휴가
까꿍 (Peekaboo)	까꿍	까꿍	까꿍	까꿍
땀 (Sweat)	땀	땀	땀	땀
뽀뽀 (Kiss)	뽀뽀	뽀뽀	뽀뽀	뽀뽀
씨앗 (Seed)	씨앗	씨앗	씨앗	씨앗
짜잔 (Ta-da!)	짜잔	짜잔	짜잔	짜잔

The second complication comes from the combination of symbols in such a way that it's difficult to tell which lines belong to which symbol. This is where the guesswork starts. The following examples walk you step-by-step through this constraint solving process.

What a cute emoticon, is it a stick figure? No, it's Hangeul, but what does it mean? Is it a combination of 'O' and '大'? Impossible, because there is no vowel. Upon closer inspection, the next possibility is the combination of 'O ㅗ ∧', forming '옷'. Even though it looks like a person, the meaning is "clothes."

Another interesting riddle: do you recognize the 'ㅜ' and the 'ㄷ'? But that doesn't make sense for the initial 'ㅣ,' as the character must start with a consonant. Thus, the only valid explanation here is 'ㄴ ㅗ ㄴ', forming '논'.

Is this character composed of 'O' followed by the double vowel 'ㅡ' combined with 'ㅏ'? If you recall your double vowels, you will remember that 'ㅡ' can only be combined with 'ㅣ', thus, that combination is impossible. The next choice is the combination of 'O ㅏ ㄱ'; is that it? There are no other choices, so that's what it is.

84

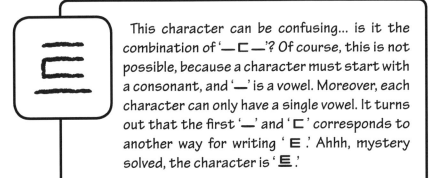

This character can be confusing... is it the combination of '— ㄷ —'? Of course, this is not possible, because a character must start with a consonant, and '—' is a vowel. Moreover, each character can only have a single vowel. It turns out that the first '—' and 'ㄷ' corresponds to another way for writing 'ㅌ.' Ahhh, mystery solved, the character is 'ㅌ.'

Fascinating indeed! Is this a 'ㅜ' combined with 'ㅍ'? But that would not work because the character cannot begin with a vowel! Thus, it is 'ㅍ' combined with 'ㅜ'. This word means "ticket." So why do Koreans write the two characters so closely together, do they love riddles? Actually, the real reason is because of aesthetics, writing the symbols closely together looks nicer, and with enough experience, there is no ambiguity at all.

This combination is indeed very tricky! Due to the proximity of 'ㅎ' and '—', it is unclear whether or not there's a dot there forming 'ㅗ'. If the dot is there, we get '화', otherwise we get 'học'. This combination can be indeed ambiguous, and you need to consider the context to be sure which one is correct.

Now, we're ready for some fun: solving a puzzle game on the next page!

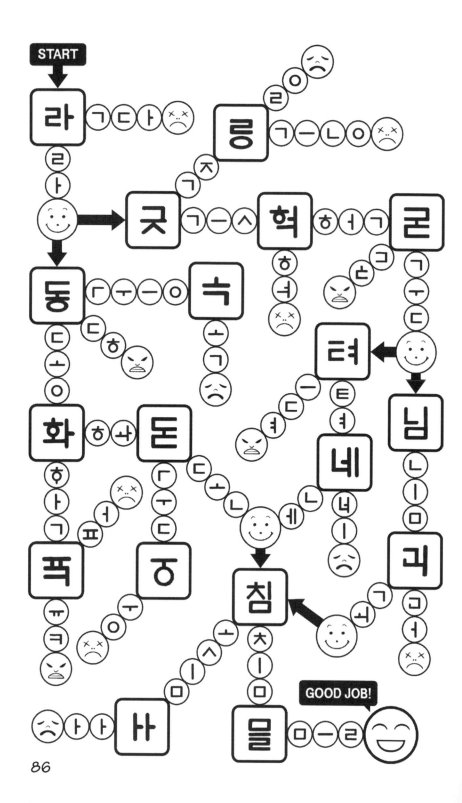

START

GOOD JOB!

86

These are some of the real examples of Hangeul on outdoor signboards. Can you guess what they mean?

리베르타 [ri-be-reu-ta]: Riberta(name)

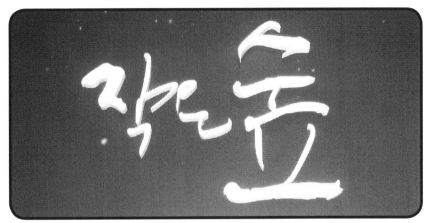

작은 숲 [jageun-sup]: small forest

다아린 갤러리 [da-a-rin gaelleo-ri]: Daarin gallery

동우 설렁탕 [dong-u seolleong-tang]: Dongwoo hot pot (beaf stew)

스타벅스 커피 [seu-ta-beok-seu keo-pi]: Starbucks coffee

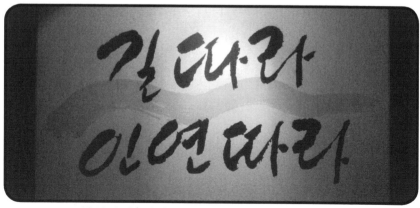

길따라 인연따라 [kil-ddara in-yeon-ddara]:
along the way, along the fate

8. HANGEUL TYPING

It is easy to enter and store Hangeul in modern computing systems.
For instance, the 12 cell-phone keys can be used for typing Hangeul,
which is much faster than typing English.

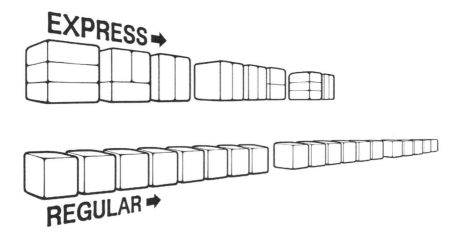

EXPRESS ➡

REGULAR ➡

In this section, we learn how to type Korean on a regular keyboard. With a short explanation, typing Korean is actually quite simple, even on cell phones! Given the expressiveness of a Korean character, a Korean SMS message is shorter than the corresponding English message. Consequently, you'll find yourself entering Korean words into SMS in no time.

(!) HANGEUL IN TWITTER

Hangeul makes the word in Alphabet shrink into a shorter format. For example, the word ' 트위터 ' [teu-wi-teo] is considered as 3 characters while 'twitter' is considered as 7 characters.

As you might know, there is a 140 character input limit in twitter, so when you want to post something longer, try using Hangeul between friends!

(1) KEYBOARD TYPING

Typing Korean on a full-size keyboard is quite natural. Below you see a depiction of the 2-Set Korean keyboard layout. To type a character, you simply compose consonants and vowels. As you type, the character is composed. For example, you can type '바나나' by pressing 'ㅂ,ㅏ,ㄴ,ㅏ,ㄴ,ㅏ.' What you see happening on the screen is quite interesting though. After the first two key presses, you see '바', but after the third you see '반', which is not what you want.

After the fourth key press, things are ok again because you see '바나', just to get messed up again after the fifth key press: '바낭.' Fortunately, the final sixth key press puts everything in order: '바나나'. What is happening is that the constraints of Hangeul are enforced as you type. Recall the rule that each vowel must be preceded by exactly one consonant? King Sejong's infinite wisdom predicted that hundreds of years later, this rule will simplify typing! Jokes aside, this indeed enables the computer to unambiguously determine word boundaries. Every time you type a vowel, the preceding consonant is taken to start the character. After typing '반' the computer does not yet know that you are going to type another vowel, so after typing 'ㅏ,' the 'ㄴ' is advanced to the next character to form '바나.' Initially, it is fun to watch the Hangeul characters dance around your screen.

Many Hangeul combinations are impossible though, such as a character with three final consonants, or inexistent double final consonants. In those cases, the computer will display a special symbol that the character does not exist, so you know you've mistyped something.

Hangeul keyboard :

An astute reader may wonder: "but wait, 14 consonants and vowels are missing!" They are formed through character combinations, the following table depicts the rules on how to type them.

ㅃ	shift + ㅂ	ㅢ	ㅡ + ㅣ
ㅉ	shift + ㅈ	ㅚ	ㅗ + ㅣ
ㄸ	shift + ㄷ	ㅟ	ㅜ + ㅣ
ㄲ	shift + ㄱ	ㅘ	ㅗ + ㅏ
ㅆ	shift + ㅅ	ㅝ	ㅜ + ㅓ
ㅒ	shift + ㅐ	ㅙ	ㅗ + ㅐ
ㅖ	shift + ㅔ	ㅞ	ㅜ + ㅔ

(2) MOBILE TYPING

Typing Hangeul on cell phones is surprisingly easy and fast! Given the regularity of consonants and vowels, the 40 symbols can be entered quickly using the 10 keys. We will explain two common methods, one used by Samsung phones, and the other by LG phones.

Although many people use smartphones with regular keyboards, learning some of the cellphone Hangeul entering methods is still useful. First, it's fun and easy! It's interesting to see the keyboard layout to minimize the number of button presses. More importantly, however, it will likely help you with some compact touchscreen keyboards with similar entering methods. For example, several Hangeul input applications optimized for smart phones (ex: Hanalgeul, Narat-geul, Milgigeul, etc.) can be learned quickly knowing Cheon Ji In and EZ Hangeul explained next.

CHEON JI IN

On Samsung phones, just three keys are used to enter all 21 vowels, and the remaining 7 keys are used for the 19 consonants. As you can see below, the consonants simply cycle through a sequence each time you press the same key. The vowels are a bit more interesting, where 1 and 3 encode the vertical and horizontal dash, respectively, and 2 encodes small dashes. By using different sequences, all vowels can be entered in a quite intuitive manner. '*, #' are not used for entering Hangeul.

ㄱ	4	ㄷ	6	ㅅ	8	ㅇ	0
ㅋ	44	ㅌ	66	ㅎ	88	ㅁ	00
ㄲ	444	ㄸ	666	ㅆ	888		
ㄴ	5	ㅂ	7	ㅈ	9		
ㄹ	55	ㅍ	77	ㅊ	99		
		ㅃ	777	ㅉ	999		

ㅣ	1	ㅣ	ㅐ	1 2 1	ㅣ · ㅣ
ㅏ	1 2	ㅣ ·	ㅒ	1 2 2 1	ㅣ · · ㅣ
ㅑ	1 2 2	ㅣ · ·	ㅔ	2 1 1	· ㅣ ㅣ
ㅓ	2 1	· ㅣ	ㅖ	2 2 1 1	· · ㅣ ㅣ
ㅕ	2 2 1	· · ㅣ	ㅚ	2 3 1	· — ㅣ
ㅗ	2 3	· —	ㅘ	2 3 1 2	· — ㅣ ·
ㅛ	2 2 3	· · —	ㅙ	2 3 1 2 1	· — ㅣ · ㅣ
ㅜ	3 2	— ·	ㅝ	3 2 1	— · ㅣ
ㅠ	3 2 2	— · ·	ㅞ	3 2 2 1	— · · ㅣ
ㅡ	3	—	ㅟ	3 2 2 1 1	— · · ㅣ ㅣ
			ㅢ	3 1	— ㅣ

EXAMPLES

바빠(busy) 7 1 2 , 7 7 7 1 2
햇살(sunshine) 8 8 1 2 1 8 , 8 1 2 5 5

COMPARE WITH ENGLISH TYPING (12-button keyboard)

Love 5 5 5 , 6 6 6 , 8 8 8 , 3 3
사랑(love) 8 1 2 , 5 5 1 2 0

Korean 5 5 , 6 6 6 , 7 7 7 , 3 3 , 2 , 6 6
한국어(Korean) 8 8 1 2 5 , 4 3 2 4 , 0 2 1

EZ HANGEUL

LG's EZ Hangeul entry method is quite different from Cheon Ji In. The '★' and '#' keys are used to cycle through different consonants and vowels. The '#' key is only used to enter the 5 double consonants, for example to enter ' ㄲ ', you first type '1' for ' ㄱ ', then type '#'. Most consonants are entered by typing a basic consonant followed by ' ★ ', as the table below indicates. For example, to type ' ㅃ ', you first enter '5' to obtain ' ㅁ ', then ' ★ ' to obtain ' ㅂ ', and finally '#' to get ' ㅃ '.

Entering vowels is a bit more intuitive. Four keys are used to enter ' ㅣ , ㅡ , ㅏ / ㅓ , ㅗ / ㅜ ', and the ' ★ ' key is used to add small dashes. More complex vowels are entered by combining several vowels. For example, to enter ' ㅐ ', you enter ' ㅗ ' followed by ' ㅏ ' and ' ㅣ ' to obtain ' ㅐ '. After a few minutes of practice, typing becomes quite mechanical. You'll certainly impress your Korean friends if you can type 한글 on your cell phone!

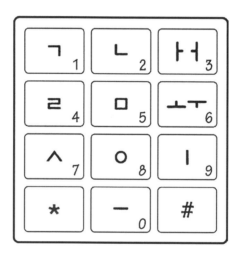

ㄱ	1	ㅋ	1*			ㄲ	1#
ㄴ	2	ㄷ	2*	ㅌ	2**	ㄸ	2*#
ㅁ	5	ㅂ	5*	ㅍ	5**	ㅃ	5*#
ㄹ	4						
ㅅ	7	ㅈ	7*	ㅊ	7**	ㅉ	7*#
ㅇ	8	ㅎ	8*			ㅆ	7#

ㅏ	3			ㅗ	6			ㅣ	9
ㅑ	3* (ㅏ*)			ㅛ	6* (ㅗ*)			ㅡ	0
ㅓ	33			ㅜ	66			ㅢ	09 ㅡㅣ
ㅕ	33* (ㅓ*)			ㅠ	66* (ㅜ*)				
ㅐ	39	ㅏㅣ	ㅚ	69 ㅗㅣ		ㅟ	669 ㅜㅣ
ㅒ	3*9	ㅑㅣ	ㅘ	63 ㅗㅏ		ㅝ	6633 ㅜㅓ
ㅔ	339	ㅓㅣ	ㅙ	639 ㅗㅏㅣ		ㅞ	66339 ㅜㅔ
ㅖ	33*9	ㅕㅣ						

EXAMPLES

바빠(busy) 5 ★ 3 , 5 ★ # 3
햇살(sunshine) 8 ★ 3 9 7 , 7 3 4

COMPARE WITH ENGLISH TYPING (12-button keyboard)

Love 5 5 5 , 6 6 6 , 8 8 8 , 3 3
사랑(love) 7 3 , 4 3 8

Korean 5 5 , 6 6 6 , 7 7 7 , 3 3 , 2 , 6 6
한국어(Korean) 8 ★ 3 2 , 1 6 6 1 , 8 3 3

Adrian Perrig

Adrian Perrig is a professor at Carnegie Mellon University. He earned his Ph.D. degree in Computer Science from Carnegie Mellon University, and spent three years during his Ph.D. degree at the University of California at Berkeley. He received his B.Sc. degree from the Swiss Federal Institute of Technology in Lausanne (EPFL). He is a recipient of the NSF CAREER award in 2004, the Sloan research fellowship in 2006, and the Benjamin Richard Teare teaching award in 2011.

Growing up in a small mountain village in Switzerland, Adrian was raised bi-lingual: his mother Heidi raised him in the Bernese Swiss German, and his father spoke the Wallis Swiss German (the dialects are quite distinct, preventing people without experience of the other to effectively communicate). In his childhood, Adrian learned High German, French, and English in primary and secondary school, and later also learned Spanish in college.

Always fascinated by Asian cultures, Adrian initially learned some Mandarin Chinese, but gave it up for the same reason King Sejong invented Hangul: studying Chinese script is a major obstacle! Greatly enjoying his visits to Korea (thanks to his intrepid and witty friend Heejo) and for communicating with his Korean friends, Adrian decided to learn Korean and was ever since hooked to master it.

Ah-yeong Yu

Ah-Yeong Yu was born in Daejeon, South Korea. She earned her bachelor's in Mechatronics from Korea University of Technology and Education. In 2012, she started her graduate studies at Sungkyunkwan University in Management of Technology. She is also working at Korea Institute of Patent Information as a patent-sleuth searching for prior art.

When she attended an English language program in Indianapolis, USA for 8 months in 2005, she was living with a very kind homestay family, who were the same age as her grand parents. The father of her homestay family was interested in Hangeul and the Korean language. He asked her to teach Korean once a week. While she was teaching him, she realized the beauty of the Korean language and felt proud of it.

Four years later, she visited Carnegie Mellon University (CMU) in Pittsburgh, USA, as a visiting researcher. She met Adrian, who is a professor at CMU. He was fascinated by Hangeul and suggested to help him edit a Korean book for foreigners to learn. Together with Heejo Lee, who is a professor at Korea University and who was also visiting CMU, the project embarked. She enjoyed the experience, especially to see the book mature when Yeon joined.

Heejo Lee

Heejo Lee is a professor at Korea University, Seoul, Korea. He received his BS, MS, Ph.D. degree from POSTECH, Pohang, Korea, and worked as a postdoc at CERIAS, Purdue University from 2000 to 2001. Before joining Korea University, he was at AhnLab, Inc. as a CTO from 2001 to 2003. When Adrian visited Korea at 2009, they found more intuitive ways of learning Korean than most other textbooks explain.

This Korean book project was further developed while Heejo was a visiting professor at CyLab/CMU, 2010. Meanwhile, he served as an advisor for cyber security in the Philippines (2006), Uzbekistan (2007), Vietnam (2009) and Myanmar (2011). The cultural experience gained in Asian and American countries gave him a chance to understand the differences between languages and to realize the need of a more intuitive textbook for foreigners to learn Korean, written from the perspective of a non-native Korean speaker.

He was grown in a peach orchard in a countryside with his parents who always supported him and became a reliable background. As the peach orchard has always been his home of good memories, he decided to dedicate this book toward his parents and the peach orchard.

Yeon Yim

Yeon Yim is a free-lance motion graphic artist. During and after earning her BFA in Visual Information from Ewha Woman's University and MFA in Film and Digital Media from Hongik University, she participated in several TV shows, commercials, games, theme parks and online services with Gamehi, Nintendo, NC Soft, MBC and MGM by making concept arts and storyboards. She was a winner of Google Korea's Best Blogger Award 2009 in Culture & Art part.

Born in Seoul, she rarely talked during her childhood so that some people thought she may be mute. Her parents, Clara and Chang, wanted to help Yeon open herself up to the world rather than just living with books and films. Thus, they traveled to different places with Yeon during her childhood. At age 14, she started challenging herself with tasks such as talking to others with more than 3 sentences, singing songs in public, or walking into a random place to introduce herself — indeed she got her first job by doing so.

With a deep interest in language learning with the power to make someone brave and overcome shyness, she gladly decided to join Adrian's Korean book project when offered by Heejo. She now wants to help others learn her native language with a smile!

ROMANIZATION TABLE

CONSONANTS

ㅇ	ㄱ	ㅋ	ㄲ	ㄴ	ㄷ	ㅌ	ㄸ	ㄹ
.	g	k	gg	n	d	t	dd	r

ㅁ	ㅂ	ㅍ	ㅃ	ㅅ	ㅆ	ㅈ	ㅊ	ㅉ	ㅎ
m	b	p	bb	s	ss	j	ch	jj	h

VOWELS

ㅏ	ㅑ	ㅓ	ㅕ	ㅣ	ㅗ	ㅛ	ㅜ	ㅠ	ㅡ
a	ya	eo	yeo	i	o	yo	u	yu	eu

ㅐ	ㅒ	ㅔ	ㅖ	ㅢ	ㅚ	ㅘ	ㅙ	ㅟ	ㅝ	ㅞ
ae	yae	e	ye	ui	oe	wa	wae	wi	wo	we

NEXT CHARACTER'S STARTING SOUND →		ㅇ	ㄱ	ㄴ	ㄷ	ㄹ	ㅁ	ㅂ	ㅅ	ㅈ	ㅊ	ㅋ	ㅌ	ㅍ	ㅎ
PREVIOUS CHARACTER'S ENDING SOUND		.	g	n	d	r	m	b	s	j	ch	k	t	p	h
ㅇ	ng	ng	ngg	ngn	ngd	ngn	ngm	ngb	ngs	ngj	ngch	ngk	ngt	ngp	ngh
ㄱ	g	g	gg	ngn	gd	ngn	ngm	gb	gs	gj	gch	gk	gt	gp	gh/k
ㄴ	n	n	ng	nn	nd	ll/nn	nm	nb	ns	nj	nch	nk	nt	np	nh
ㄷ	t	d/j	tg	nn	td	nn	nm	tb	ts	tj	tch	tk	tt	tp	t/ch
ㄹ	l	r	lg	ll	ld	ll	lm	lb	ls	lj	lch	lk	lt	lp	lh
ㅁ	m	m	mg	mn	md	mn	mm	mb	ms	mj	mch	mk	mt	mp	mh
ㅂ	p	b	pg	mn	pd	mn	mm	pb	ps	pj	pch	pk	pt	pp	ph/p

3418110R00056

Printed in Great Britain
by Amazon.co.uk, Ltd.,
Marston Gate.